A Life Behind Bars

by Fabian Harper

iUniverse, Inc.
New York   Bloomington

A Life Behind Bars

by Fabian Harper

A Life Behind Bars

iUniverse books may be ordered through booksellers or by contacting:

iUniverse
1663 Liberty Drive
Bloomington, IN 47403
www.iuniverse.com
1-800-Authors (1-800-288-4677)

ISBN: 978-1-4401-4260-4 (pbk)
ISBN: 978-1-4401-4259-8 (ebk)

Printed in the United States of America

Front cover photo courtesy of the author

Preface

I am in prison for being principal to murder, serving a sentence of life in prison without parole. At the time of arrest I was 16. The circumstances that led to my imprisonment are complicated and sad. The person who pulled the trigger received seven years to testify I was with him, and I was convicted and sentenced to life. October 2009 will mark my eighteenth year in prison, two more years than when I was free. These years have marked for me a long struggle toward faith and self discovery. There are many good volunteer chaplains, prison administrators, and family members who have helped me become the man I am today

It is often said that you never understand a man until you walk a mile in his shoes. I invite you in these pages to walk through the daily sights and sounds of Angola Prison, to witness the hurt and loneliness of doing time. It is a process of getting up every day and finding a reason to hope. It is a daily discipline of struggles and reassurances, of doubts and faith. Over time prisoners struggle to get adjusted, but most never adjust. My shoes are not ones I would wish on anybody. I share what little wisdom and experience God has given me with the hope that, as you read these pages, my life can offer you insight into the choices you will make.

Prologue

Behind trees, way back in the Louisiana Tunica Hills, is the small town of Angola. On the town's land are a hospital, ambulances, a fire station, and houses of families. There is a lake, with a ramp to lower boats so the townsfolk can fish. On clear summer days the town's children will play softball in their little ballpark, while their parents are on the golf course greens playing golf. And when the afternoons are hot, the whole town will meet at the town swimming pool; the children will splash around in the water as their mothers sit tanning and the fathers drink beer and barbeque. If you ask the people living in the town, they will say that Angola is the best place in the world to live. But if you drive a little further through the town, down a five-mile stretch of asphalt road, you will find men kept separate from the townspeople by brick and fences. They are the prisoners of Angola, of which I am one.

Coming to the end of that black road you will see scores of prisoners walking around a grass yard behind fences and barbed wire. The large block dormitories where they sleep lie behind them. Behind and on the sides of the dorms are acres upon acres of fields planted with vegetables. A bright hot sun seems to always hang over those fields. And a stinky odor of horse manure from a nearby pasture constantly lingers in the air.

I and other prisoners are marched from our dorms in the sun to the vegetable fields. The fields look like endless rows of green, white, and purple that appear to meet the sky in the distance. Just looking at the field rows angers me. Every now and then while in the fields I gaze out beyond the fields. An outline of a dense forest is far off circling around the land, and a grassy levee that holds back the Mississippi River traces the bottom of the trees. Sometimes I even see the children racing their dirt bikes or trucks up the levee yelling out "Wahoo's" and townsfolk driving past, honking their horns and waving at the guards watching us. And when it is time to go back to our dorms, we walk past the lake filled with people sitting in their boats fishing. Some will wave and others will continue casting their lines.

To the Angola townsfolk, this place is home. But beneath their cheerfulness and laughter is the knowledge that we are nearby. As they look toward the field and see prisoners bent over picking vegetables under a hot sun while guards sit on horseback watching, they always know, as do we, that Angola is a prison.

Chapter 1

I was standing outside Hunt Correctional Center near Baton Rouge on a crisp Louisiana morning. Chained to me were five other men. We watched as a yellow bus pulled into the parking lot and stopped. It was the Angola transport bus. The door opened and a guard stepped out and nodded to the Hunt guard who was standing with us.

"The white jumpsuits mine?" he asked, pointing at us.

The Hunt guard responded, "Yep," and handed him some papers to sign.

After the Angola guard gave the papers back, he looked at us and said, "Follow me."

In a line, we walked behind him to the bus where he pointed up the steps, which we went up one at a time. We had shackles on our ankles, so walking down the bus's narrow aisle was slow; however, the chains around our wrists had enough slack to stretch over the back of the seats, allowing each of us to sit by ourselves. The other prisoners sat together; I sat alone.

I sat on the green plastic seat and stared out the window. As the bus pulled out of the parking lot and turned onto a road that ran through the small town of St. Gabriel, I slid down the seat by the window and stared out at houses, people walking, and cars passing. The way the bus bounced and squeaked over bumps in the road reminded me of when I used to ride a bus to school. Only the bus I was on now wasn't taking me to school—it was taking me to prison.

The drive to Angola took less than an hour and a half. The bus drove down a road that ran through the dense forest of West Feliciana Parish past wood frame houses and broken-down trailers, then turned off on an asphalt road that snaked around grassy dirt hills until a big green sign warning "You are entering prison grounds" came in sight. During the ride I was so immersed in my thoughts that before I realized it, the bus had passed through the prison's front gate and was parked in front of a large building.

"Welcome to Angola!" the guard said as he opened the bus door.

Another Angola guard came out of the building to meet the bus. He ordered us off and we filed off the bus slowly. The guard told us to follow him into the building. As I was walking through the entrance door I looked up at the building and understood where I was. The building was the Reception Center. For decades it had stood, its walls painted beige—and though I don't believe it was by intent, those beige walls made the building appear cold, plain, dead.

Inside the Reception Center we were put in a cell together to wait. It was an empty space about the length and width of a boxing ring. There was, at least, a low gray-matted bench pushed against the wall for us to sit on. I remember Raymond, who sat behind me on the bus, with his eyes wide and his body stiff on the bench. It doesn't matter how tough you are; it's still hard not to be scared when you are sitting there waiting for your fate to be determined in a strange place. In the parish jail you hear the horror stories that I imagined Raymond must have been thinking about.

I was sitting there quietly when he nudged me with his elbow. "I ain't doing no life sentence," he said. I knew exactly how he felt. When you first ride through Angola's front gate, you think that you will go back out as easily as you came in. The truth is, many men have come through that gate with the same optimism, but that dream was seldom realized. Traveling down that back road to get to Angola was the last time they saw freedom. They died within these walls. And now there were six of us who sat on that same bench when the guard came to tell us, "Come on, it's time for lunch."

Still chained together, we walked in a line past a dark monitor room, by an inmate law library, into an empty kitchen. The only people waiting for us in the dining hall were two guards and three prisoners to serve our food. They wore white cloth caps, white short sleeved shirts, and white pants, pressed to a crease, sparkling like the stainless steel tables where we ate. Our meal was a large spoon of red beans spread over a small pile of white rice. Everyone was quiet. The only sounds in the kitchen were our tin spoons scraping up beans out of the metal plates.

After we finished eating, the guard who had escorted us to the kitchen said to us, "Time to go get your picture taken, boys."

We got up from the table and followed him down a hallway to double iron doors. When he leaned his body into the doors, pushing them open, a gust of hot air hit each of us in the face. The guard led us into a low-ceilinged corridor. It was a good thing that the chains on our wrists had enough slack between us so that we could walk behind one another, because that corridor was too narrow for two average-sized men to walk side by side. The corridor's floor slanted downward, ramp-like, leading to the building's basement where the ID room was. That corridor was dark. I will never forget my heart racing as I walked down that black hallway, trying to feel my way as I had done when I walked around in the dark at home, touching nothing—until up ahead, we saw a light shining bright out of the door of the ID room, marking the end of our short journey. It was almost like we had died and were traveling to a life on the other side. In truth, we were entering a new world where we would never again live our lives on our own terms. Everything would be decided for us—where to go, what to eat, and when to sleep.

The ID room was the size of a home bathroom. Only a fingerprint table, camera, and photographer's lamp could be seen when we first walked in. Then I saw an inmate standing quietly in the corner behind a barber's chair, holding a pair of electric clippers.

"Before I take your pictures," the guard said, "you gots to get your hair cut."

We looked at each other, not saying a word.

I sat in the chair first. Within moments, I heard the low noise of the clippers buzzing on my head, taking clumps of hair off at a time. Bzz, bzzz, bz, done. It took less than three minutes to shave all six of our heads practically bald; then we were finger-printed and took turns facing front, then side, for the guard flicking our pictures.

After taking our pictures, the guard escorted us back up the corridor, out the double doors, back down the hall, and into a shower stall. There were six sprinkler heads, one for each of us.

"Strip naked," we were told, "and put all your personal clothing out by the door."

We shed the last things we owned: those white t-shirts, socks, and underwear that symbolized what we claimed as ours were taken from us and piled on the floor outside the shower. From now on, we would own nothing unless they gave it to us, but by then, it would not be ours to own. They can come and take it back at a moment's notice.

Standing there naked, I shivered slightly. As I stood in that shower waiting for the next instruction, it was hard not to feel awkward, look-ing into the eyes of a total stranger, staring back at my nude body, without shifting to one side a little and folding my arms across my chest—that was exactly the posture I took.

"Turn around," the guard said, looking at us. "Turn around and spread your legs, then bend over, grab both of your buttcheeks, and spread 'em apart so I can see your asshole, and cough."

"WHAT?" was my first reaction. But if I didn't comply, several big bodyguards would only wrestle me to the ground and forcibly pull apart my buttocks. I didn't want that to happen. I turned around with everyone else, bending over to pull open my cheeks, when I realized that I had no control over myself. I had to now do everything demanded of me with no questions of what I thought. I was their property now, and the quicker I understood this, they told me, the easier it would be.

When the guard finished looking in every hole and between every crack of our bodies, he stepped out of the shower and a prisoner walked in carrying a skinny black hose connected to a knee-tall pesticide container he carried in his other hand. He set the cylinder-shaped container down on the shower floor and pulled up a lever attached to a metal rod inside the container, then pushed it back down, pumping air into it.

"Close ya'll eyes," the prisoner told us, "and lift your arms." He then began spraying the front of our naked bodies with a mist of lice pesticide.

"Turn around."

We did. And he covered our backs, legs, and butts with the spray. After being sprayed, the shower water came on for us to rinse the pesticide from our bodies and hair. There were no curtains or partition walls in the shower. We showered naked beside each other, and as the water ran down my face and back, it hit me that the privacy I once enjoyed was no more. Every shower that I took, every time I raised my shirt and exposed my naked butt to sit on the toilet would always be in the presence of other prisoners' peeping eyes.

Once we finished showering, the guard gave us a white towel to dry off. Then he told us to put on a pair of jeans and blue shirt that were folded neatly on a table across from the shower.

He then led us to a room where two classification officers and a guard sat behind a table waiting for us to arrive. They were there to evaluate us. We took turns sitting at the table across from them, answering their questions.

"You have any children?"

"Yes."

"What's your religion?"

"Baptist."

"You ever done time before?"

"No."

This whole process was quick. It took that small board less than five minutes to interview all six of us. During that period they decided to house us all in a working cellblock. Their reasoning for that assignment was since the six of us were all under the age of twenty-one and had never been incarcerated before, the cellblock offered us the best opportunity to adjust to prison life. Having never experienced the cellblock as a young prisoner, I can say that it was the worst place prison officials could have sent us. In the cellblocks are housed many seasoned prisoners with predatory minds. They intentionally stay there waiting patiently, hoping that a young unsuspecting prisoner like I was would to be sent to their cell. They are master manipulators of the prison system in keeping their cell open during that entire period of lingering. Finally, when a new prisoner comes into their cell, they call it a "catch," a term that I later identified with the "Fresh Fish" title old prisoners gave us new prisoners.

Before leaving the evaluators, the classification officer handed me an identification card.

"Keep this with you at all times," he said, and I took the card from his hand. The card was a small picture of my face with the numbers 33 63 74 above my head. I couldn't help but think that the number was now my name, that I was only a number now. If prison guards wanted to call me they would recite the number aloud. If they wanted to give me mail or let me make a phone call, I would have to repeat the number. This fact made me feel less human, like a piece of tagged livestock.

I walked out of the room with the other new prisoners.

Every Thursday was Fresh Fish day, the day new prisoners were escorted in a single line from a walkway to their classified housing. The walkway runs between four cellblocks, and homosexuals, penitentiary pimps, and hardened criminals stood on the block's recreation yards behind rusted fences on both sides of the walk. They were smiling, their eyes bright with excitement, whispering to one another, pointing at us, trying to pick which of us would be their prey.

I was barely twenty years old that day. I walked down that walkway on display with the other new prisoners just before the sun would disappear for the day—staying in line close behind Raymond, quiet, looking at those prisoners behind those fences as if I were a child on a school field trip. It seemed like there were a thousand men on those rec yards, standing close to those fences and watching us pass. I could feel their eyes staring at us like we were fashion models in bikinis.

"Tell them to put you in this block," one of them shouted.

"Don't give it to nobody, wait for me," another one said.

It was impossible to tell who hollered at us. I kept walking, my head straight. I had never been to penitentiary before, but I had enough sense to know that it was too late to act scared. I knew everything I said or did would count.

Cellblock C had a cell that was completely empty. By luck, Raymond and I were assigned to it while the other four new prisoners were placed in cells with other prisoners. When I walked into the cell, I looked around at how small it was. I stood in the center of the floor and stretched out my arms. I could touch both of the cell's side walls with my finger tips. Besides iron bunk beds that were bolted to the wall, the cell had only a face bowl with a steel toilet mounted on the wall below it next to the bottom bunk. Raymond asked me which bed I wanted, and I chose the top bunk. Because there was no ladder that I could use to climb into the bunk, I had to step on the toilet seat, then onto the corner of the face bowl, which I leaped from into the bed.

I sat straight in my bed with my feet hanging off the side and looked around at the cell: the red-painted bars, the cracks in the concrete floor, and the walls. Those walls. Those white-painted walls. That is what my life had been reduced to—walls. I shook my head. Then I reached for the white trash bag that the classification officer gave each of us during our evaluations. In the bag were two extra pairs of jeans, three blue shirts, a couple t-shirts and boxers, some socks, and the few letters, pictures, and books they let me keep from Hunt. I dug around in the bag for a letter my mother wrote me soon after I was convicted. I unfolded it and read her words again.

March 1, 1994

Dear Fabian,

Today is another day that I wake up and wish you were here. I still can't believe what all has happened. You are my only son, and I can't help but feel you have been taken from me. Often I have asked myself where did I go wrong, or what I could have done differently or better in raising you. Maybe if I had been there for you more. I feel like I failed you. If only I could have gotten you to understand, if only I had gotten you to see before this. I ask God to give me strength and to see his purpose through this, but honestly, I am struggling with the reality you are gone, and I asked why.

I know that you told me that you are innocent and I believe you, but that doesn't comfort me. The fact that you are not here with me so I can see you, hug you, even fuss at you, is what's hurting. And this pain I feel won't ever go away. I will walk with it every day until you're home.

I know you thought that you didn't matter to me, but that was the furthest from the truth. I love you, Fabian; no matter what you are still my son. I cry for you. That's what mothers do when one of their children gone. But all I can do now is cry for you; you are in God's hands. I just ask him to bring me back to you safely.

Love,

Your mother

Tracy Harper

After I read her letter, I sat there holding it for a few minutes. Tears had come into my eyes, not because I was locked in a concrete cell, though that was hurting, but because I realized the pain I had brought on my family. They would suffer with me. No matter if I didn't want them to care, they would.

I folded the letter back up and went to sleep.

The next morning, after Raymond and I took turns brushing our teeth, I sat on his bed waiting for breakfast. A prisoner walked down the hall carrying four trays. Like a waiter, he held two trays in each hand as he passed our cell going to the cell next door. He then came to our cell and did the same.

As Raymond and I ate, the prisoner who had brought our tray stood outside our cell watching us, and I started feeling that he was studying us, trying to discern our attitudes. Then he told us that the cell block guard said to be dressed for the hospital.

"Every new prisoner see the doctor when they first get here," he told us, "to see if you got any health problems or need a work duty status."

I stopped eating and glared up at him. He appeared to be in his mid-forties, clean-shaven. His face was shiny with grease, and I recognized that same excited look in his black eyes that I saw in those faces behind the fences when we came down the walkway. I said nothing.

Then he asked, "What's ya'll name?"

"Why?" I snapped, then cut my eyes to Raymond. He kept eating.

"Oh, OK," he said. "Well ya'll need to hurry and eat 'cause the guard will be opening the cell doors soon." Then he went up the tier.

When he left, I knew that he presented a fact I would have to face, proving that I was not going to be fucked.

A guard came and walked me and Raymond to the hospital. Once there, it took a doctor less than two minutes to give us a physical and declare we were as fit as "two horses." He then gave Raymond and me a card that said, "regular duty."

When Raymond and I got back to the block, the other prisoners had come in from working in the field and were in their cells waiting on lunch. All of the TV's on the tier were turned to The Price is Right. Bob Barker was helping a short old lady spin the big wheel.

Going back to my cell, I walked down the tier, cutting my eyes at prisoners in their cells. Some of them had pulled their locker boxes from under their beds close to the doors and were sitting on them watching television, while others were stretched out on the floor asleep. My eyes caught a few of their eyes staring at me and I wondered what they were thinking about me and Raymond, who was walking behind me with a bounce and glide in his steps, trying to give an impression he was hip.

Back in our cell, a prisoner brought Raymond and me our lunch trays. We were fed a scoop of instant potatoes, a soybean meat patty, a roll, and jello. When the hospital guard brought us back to the block, the block guard who let us in told Raymond and me to be ready for work duty when our cell opened at noon. So I hurried to eat my meal, taking large bites from the roll, stuffing my mouth full of potatoes, and swallowing half-chewed meat. I didn't touch the jello.

It was 12:00 p.m. when all the televisions went off. "Work Call," I heard the block guard holler down the hall. There was a low electrical buzz, a pop, and then all of the cell doors simultaneously slammed back. Men quickly came out of their cells, some of them carrying their work boots in their hands. Raymond and I were unfamiliar with this hasty procedure, and our cell door quickly closed back with us still in the cell. One of the prisoners hollered to the guard at the front tier who was controlling the doors: "Say, you locked the fresh fishes in." Our door opened again and Raymond and I came out of our cell onto the tier with the other prisoners.

When we made it to the front of the tier heading outdoors, the block guard told Raymond and me that was our warning.

"Don't ever get caught in your cell again," he said. "When your cell doors open, you best be standing at your door ready to step out, or you'll find yourselves across the hall in the hole, understand."

We nodded obediently

Outside, the rays from the afternoon sun stung my eyes so much that I had to squint them as I scanned the open recreation yard. As my eyes adjusted to the sunlight, I saw bunches of prisoners walking fast toward a large fenced area that resembled a gladiator's cage. There were prison guards walking behind the prisoners just as fast, blowing whistles and hollering at them to hurry to get inside the cage. I stood there stiff, watching the whole scene, not really believing what my eyes were taking in when, before I knew it, a prison guard was upon me spitting on the side of my face as he yelled in my ear to get walking to the cage. Like cattle drivers directing a herd of cows through a gate into a pasture, the guards were walking behind us into a fenced-in ground called the Bullpen.

The Bullpen was a flat of clear dirt ground that had four ten-foot tall fences constructed around it, forming a large rectangle. The fences looked new. As they flapped in the light breeze, sun rays reflected off their silver coating like a mirror into my eyes so that my eyelids instinctively shut to block the bright rays from my eyes. Coiled around the top of the fences was barbed wire that did not have the same look of newness that the fences had. It was weather-beaten, dull, and corroded stiff with rust.

As we walked through the Bullpen's entrance gate, the dirt ground was cement hard, with small dirt clumps and holes. Baked into the ground by the sun were two straight footpaths that stretched from the back of the pen to its front.

I stood in the Bullpen with the other prisoners. It was noisy. Prisoners were trying to talk over each other. We were so crowded together that I could hardly move or turn. I couldn't feel any breeze because we were so bunched together I became nauseated from smelling the prisoners' funky bodies every time I breathed in. I was so nervous that my heart pounded and I was sweating hard. I stood close to the Bullpen's front exit so the guards that were outside the pen on horseback could see me. Only one prisoner stood in front of me; he was a white man who appeared to be in his mid forties. The sun had turned his skin to a strawberry red, and his bald head was peeling flakes of skin, but I imagined that if he had hair it would have been the color of his mingled gray and black handlebar moustache and bushy eyebrows. His blue jeans were worn white at the thighs and he wore a v-neck t-shirt that had turned a dingy white , with a pack of Camel cigarettes rolled up into the sleeve. I read the tattoo on his arm.

"Cow Rustler," I said low. He turned to look at me.

"All fishes line up in the back," he told me. "Only older cons up here."

His deep voice inside the pen made me shake and tremble. Though I was unsure if Cow Rustler was telling me right, I began making my way toward the back of the pen, squeezing my way through prisoners, big, tall, short, wide, black, white, some with shaggy hair braided hair, or short hair—and they all stared down at me as I politely said, "Excuse me," prying myself between them. As I got close to the Bullpen's rear, I noticed that prisoners' faces kept getting younger. "Cow Rustler didn't lie," I thought.

The heat from the sun was aggravatingly hot. Sweat ran down my back and forehead, and wiping it away, I wondered how the prisoners standing around me could be cheerful. They were laughing and talking to each other as if the sun didn't bother them. I then looked through the fence holes and saw other prisoners laughing as they made their way inside the pen. A few of them were even smiling and joking with a guard as he slammed the gate shut. Observing this gave me the impression that working in the fields was not going to be that hard, that we were going to go out there and do some light work, then go back inside. I learned, however, that field work was hell.

The guard who had closed the gate took a set of iron skeleton keys from his side, chose one, then stuck it into the gate latch, locking it. He then turned to us.

"Hold the noise down!" he hollered. "Deuce it up and listen for your number."

Slowly the men's talking voices faded to low murmurs, and in several seconds it was completely quiet, except for the guard saying, "Get out of my way," as he shoved his way through the prisoners. When he got to the front of the Bullpen, he pulled open the pen's front gate. Eight older prisoners then walked out of the gate past the guard and across a narrow dirt road to a small outhouse-looking wood shack. That was where all the field tools were kept. Those who went to the shack, I learned, were part of what was called the Headline Crew. Each cellblock has its own set of Headliners. The only jobs in the field were to take the field tools from the shack, walk the lines of prisoners out to different areas of the field and once out there, assign each prisoner a portion of the field to work. In my line, three of the Headliners had on jeans that fitted like spandex, and tied on their heads were pink, yellow, and red bandanas. They were prison queens. They slung their hips side to side as they walked across the road to the shack to help the other five Headliners take out some field hoes and lay them on the ground. No queen worked the fields, I learned. Prisoners who weren't queens were considered "the men," and they saw queens as women; thus the queens were viewed as weaker vessels. It's not that queens couldn't work, but since they were looked at as women, it was considered disrespectful to a "man" for a queen to outwork him. If a queen tried working as a man, he was seen as rebellious and this usually ended in quarrels or fights. So to maintain a smooth operation of his line, the guard who was in charge of getting work done in the field didn't allow queens to work. In fact, no prison whores, prostitutes, wives, or sneak freaks did any work in the fields. They either stood and flirted with the men prisoners as they worked, or they helped their "man," whom they were married to. I came to see the use of those prison homosexuals as one of the many psychological devices prison guards use to control the temperament of the prison population.

"Listen up!" the Bullpen guard hollered from the front of the pen. He held a metal clipboard with some papers clamped to it. "When I call your prison number, walk through this gate answering, go pick up a hoe, and pair off in line."

This would be our routine each morning: to walk through the gate answering, "Yeah," to our number being called, then cross the dirt road to pick up a hoe that the Headliner had laid in the grass next to the shack, then, stand next to each other on the dirt road in two paired lines.

I was in the first line to go out the gate, line one, the hardest working line in the prison. Line one was used to break in all new prisoners and to punish troublemakers from other lines. The line pusher, a guard who was in charge of working our line, sat on a horse outside the Bullpen watching us walk through the gate after we answered to our number.

My number was finally called.

"33 63 74."

"Yeah!" I spoke out, then walked through the gate to go get a hoe when the line pusher stopped me.

"Say."

I stopped and looked up at him. I read his name tag, "Beverly." But prisoners who worked in his line, the one I was now in, called him "Pharaoh." He appeared to be about thirty-five. The sun had turned his brown skin black as coal. He wore military fatigues. Looking at him, I instantly became angry because he was a black man willing to work his line of black prisoners in that heat.

He leaned halfway off the side of his horse and spat a shot of tobacco in the dirt, then looking at me, asked, "You just got here?"

I stared at him with an expression that said, "Duh, stupid." I knew he recognized my new-prisoner appearance: the low haircut, the stiff new jeans, a blue shirt, and the brown leather brogans on my feet.

"You gonna answer me," he said.

"Yeah," I snapped. "I just came to this plantation."

My sharp response caught him off guard because I saw his eyebrows rise. He then straightened his back in his saddle and took a deep breath.

"Consider yourself fortunate," he said. "Now go get in line."

"What do you mean, fortunate?" I shot back. "There ain't nothing fortunate about being locked up."

He gave me a false smile and seemed to chuckle a little to himself.

"Sorry you feel that way," and then he narrowed his eyes at me. "Now get in line!"

"What if I don't," I snapped again. "What you gonna do, I'm already locked up."

A look of agitation came on his face. It was Friday, the last day of work before the weekend, and no prisoner in his right mind wanted to spend the weekend in administrative segregation, known among prisoners as "the hole."

He grinned. "I see you gonna have a lot of fun." Then he walked his horse through the line of prisoners. As I stared at his back swaying in the horse's saddle, I wished my eyes could have knocked him right out of it. I went to pick up a hoe and glanced over at the line of prisoners. Some of them appeared shocked. It was as if they had never witnessed anyone talking to Beverly the way I had and was surprised I did. I learned later from some of the prisoners in the line that my defiance was normal. They were only surprised that Beverly didn't send me to the hole. Then they gave me this advice: "Watch yourself, 'cause he's gonna get you."

Line One had a bunch of young prisoners my age who looked like typical high school kids. Though the sun had aged their faces, I could still spot their youthful innocence underneath layers of dust and sun-burned skin. Clearly they were not as tough as they wanted to appear to be. They were children like me who had made too many mistakes.

The sun seemed to get hotter as I stood in line, holding the hoe against my shoulder, waiting for us to start walking. Beverly slowly walked his horse down the line counting us. When he got to the front next to the Headliners, he hollered out, "Walk it!" and we started to move.

It was 12:30 and that sun was hot. Having to stay close to Beverly's horse, we walked at a brisk pace side by side down that dirt road. At times I wondered if I was going to make it. I kept praying for a cloud to come and cover the sun, but none ever appeared. I could feel my boots' stiff leather rubbing against the soft skin of my feet and sweat running down my face, legs, and arms. The heat felt like it was choking me as I labored to breathe.

"Walk it up!" a gun guard on his horse behind us hollered.

"Get that gap out of the line!" came another shout.

Prisoners mumbled that they were tired and needed a break, but there would be none. We would not stop until we reached our work site. We walked down that road, cut through a field of dried soybeans, jumped over a sewerage ditch to get on another dirt road that we walked down kicking up dirt, until a dried-up tomato field soon came in sight.

When we stopped in front of the field of withered tomato plants, some of the prisoners put their hoes down and leaned on them to rest. Beverly hollered, "Keep your tools in the air and stay lined up." He then pulled from his saddle bag some papers stapled together. They were a roster of our names. While we stood there waiting for Beverly, an old prisoner riding in a wagon pulled by two mules stopped next to us. I wondered where he came from because I did not see him anywhere when we walked up to the field. It was as if he just dropped out of the sky. On the wagon were ten 50 gallon yellow Igloo coolers filled with water. Two Headliners took four of the coolers from the bed of the wagon and sat them on the ground. The old prisoner then tugged at the leather straps attached to the mules for them to pull the wagon on. Beverly was now ready.

"Listen up for your cut number," he shouted. A cut number is when the Headliner calls out a number after the line pusher yells out our names. The number helps the line pusher keep track of who is or isn't working in the line. It is the Headliner's responsibility to keep track of who has what number, so if the line pusher inspects each cut and is not satisfied, he can ask his Headliner whose cut it was.

"Williams!" hollered Beverly.

"One," a worker said after him.

"Young!"

"Two."

"Whitehead!"

"Three," and so it went until Beverly had called out every prisoner's name. My number was 50, the last number.

Then Beverly said, "I want this field scraped tight. Chop everything down. I don't want to see one blade of grass sticking up from the ground. Pull all your slack to the end of the field and spread it out. Don't leave none of it piled up." He then told the Headliner, "Set 'em in."

"How many steps, boss?" asked the Headliner.

"Fifteen and one," responded Beverly.

We were still lined up behind the Headliner with our hoes in the air, when he started taking steps, counting off fifteen paces, then stopping to scrape a line in the ground with his hoe.

Cut one!" he yelled. He then walked off another fifteen steps and marked another line in the ground. "Cut two!"

For each number that he called, a prisoner stepped out of the line in between the markers and started chopping down the dead plants and wild weeds. By the time the headline had finished counting off all our cuts, we were stretched all across the one-acre tomato field.

I began to cut down the plants that were in my cut. The sun was bright and its rays struck the back of my neck as I bent over the hoe, chopping at the base of the plants. The vibration of the hoe's wooden handle from hitting the blade against the hard field dirt rubbed a blister on my thumb, and streams of sweat from my forehead dripped into my eyes as I grunted to pull out the plants' roots with my hoe.

"Headline!" Beverly shouted. The afternoon work half was now over.

We lined up and started our walk back to the prison. Though Beverly knew we were exhausted from working, he galloped his horse on ahead, making us walk back just as fast as we had walked out to the field. The Bullpen soon came into view along with the cellblock. I could see prisoners who had already made it in walking around the recreation yard talking.

We made it to the Bullpen; the gate was already opened for us to walk through.

I slowly walked back to my cell and sat on the floor beside Raymond's bed. He had already flopped down. I carefully pulled off my boots, then my socks, and I saw where the boots' stiff leather had rubbed maroon blisters on my heels and big toes. The heat of the afternoon together with the pace in which we walked and worked had gotten to me. I leaned my head back against the rail of the bed, closed my eyes and waited for supper.

After supper, the door opened for the evening yard call. Raymond and I went on the recreation yard with the other prisoners housed in the cellblock. I kept to myself, but Raymond mingled with some of the older prisoners, and over the next few weeks, he began to drift away from me. He soon started spending this leisure time in the company of Black Boy, who controlled most of the gambling in the cellblock and was the store man, a prisoner who sold canteen food items out of his cell for cigarettes or for a promise to pay back a higher interest on canteen day. Within those few weeks, Raymond started staying in the cell when the doors opened for us to go on the yard so he could shower with Black Boy. Everyone knew why Raymond started taking his showers with Black Boy. Raymond had become a canteen whore, someone who literally exchanged sex for food items or a few minor luxuries that anyone would give him.

Raymond was not homosexual, and I doubt he enjoyed the hours lying on his stomach getting screwed in his butt or on his knees sucking men off. But he had given in to what a lot of prisoners before him had, wanting to live the penitentiary "high life." Being able to walk around in pressed Levi jeans instead of state blues, to eat foods purchased from the canteen and not have to eat kitchen food, to wear high-priced sneakers and boots is considered among prisoners "living good," and this philosophy drives many prisoners who are trying to find some semblance of normalcy inside prison. Such living earns a high status among his peers. And since Raymond desired to be in that social order but had no steady outside financial support to sustain the prison's "high life," he auctioned off the only thing that could bring him money, his body. Raymond's sexual services soon became my problem.

Black Boy had fallen in love with Raymond and was pressuring him to move out of the cell with me and down into the cell with him. Raymond told me privately that he didn't want to move, but he kept giving Black Boy the excuse that he didn't know how to get a cell change. Finally Black Boy came up with a plan that involved me.

While I had my arms folded in the rec yard, watching some prisoners play a game of basketball, Black Boy walked past me, stopped, looked sharply as if trying to think who I was, and then approached.

"Say Fabe," he said. "I need to run something at you."

"Shoot," I said.

"You know that's my little people in the cell with you." I nodded. "You see, he really want to get in the cell with me, but the people ain't gonna just move him."

"What's that got to do with me?"

"Well, I told him since ya'll cool he could ask you to tell the people ya'll don't get along."

"What?"

"Be cool, they ain't gonna mess with you," he said. "Raymond will tell them that ya'll been having words and they will ask him who he can live with and he's gonna say me. Then they will swap me and you out."

I gave Black Boy one of my "Are you crazy?" looks.

"What you say? You'll do it?"

I was blunt. "No."

"Why?"

" 'Cause…"

He said nothing more and walked off, but the next evening on the rec yard, he approached me and said, "Hey, man, you gonna move or what?"

"What?"

"Huh?"

"You said 'or what' to me. What does that mean?"

"Are you gonna move?"

"No."

He stared at me. "We'll see," he murmured, turning to walk away. "I bet you get out of that cell."

That night in my cell I didn't say anything to Raymond. I was upset at him for putting me in the middle of him and Black Boy. Then I decided that the best thing for me was to get a cell change, but I wasn't going to go in the cell with Black Boy's celly. There was a bed open in a cell down the hall. I decided to ask the block guard to move me in there. But before I could make my request, the next afternoon when I came in from work for lunch, the block guard handed me a white jumpsuit to put on.

"For what?" I asked.

"We found a knife underneath your pillow." He said.

"What? A knife?" Then it hit me; I had been set up.

I went before the disciplinary board and tried to explain how I couldn't have had a knife.

"I just got here," I said. "How could I know where to get a knife from?"

But they didn't hear me. Presenting the board with logic and common sense never works, I would learn. I was re-classified to segregation lockdown, Camp J.

Chapter 2

On the day I was transferred to Camp J, the hole guard woke me in the morning, told me to pack up everything, and be ready to roll out. The oddest thing I remember of walking past those Camp J prisoner cells on my way to mine was that they were all asleep. I wondered why, and after being there a few days, I figured out that the night times were day for many of the prisoners that lived back there. I emphasize the words "lived back there" because there is a distinction to be made between prisoners who came there to do their disciplinary confinement and those prisoners who lived in those cells. The prisoners, of which I was one, went there to serve their punishment, do their year or so of solitary confinement, and leave. However, prisoners who lived in those cells do not want to leave; there are many there with that attitude. They are known as Camp J Warriors. At night these prisoners are up shaking their cell doors, arguing with each other, shouting in their cell air vent at the cell behind them, and throwing their body waste on the tier at one another. When I was in the hole, a prisoner who brought me my food said, "Don't get caught up back there. Just stay to yourself. They got guys who love it back there and will use you up." I took his advice and kept quiet. I learned to sleep through the noise those prisoners made, but occasionally I would lie in my bed and listen to them yell at each other.

"Nigga, you ain't shit!" the prisoner in one cell hollered.

A prisoner in cell 12 yelled back, "Fuck you!"

"Nigga, suck my ____!"

"Say!" a guard would shout from the front of the tier. "Shut up!"

"Fuck you!" one of the prisoners hollered out.

All night long insults like this would be shouted up and down the tier. Occasionally, I laughed at some of their comments, and there were times I sat on my bed cursing them for being what I called stupid. But what more could I really expect of these prisoners? There was nothing to do at Camp J. You were only let out of your cell for fifteen minutes each day to shower. For the rest of the nearly 23½ hours you were locked in that cell by yourself; you just sat on your bed and stared at nothing. There were no TV's, no radios, no chessboards to help pass the time. Occasionally, when the prison librarian passed with his squeaky cart, I would get a book to read. But for most of my time when I first got there, if I wasn't asleep, I would lie in my bed and stare at the cell's blank walls. My solitude was disturbed one day, however, when the prisoner in the cell next to me stuck his arm out of his bars and tapped on mine.

"Say!" he called. "You 'wake over there?"

I pretended not to hear him. Up to then no one had bothered me, and I didn't talk to anyone because talking usually ended in arguments. He tapped on my bars again.

"Say! You hear me?"

When after a few more taps I didn't respond, he pulled his hand back. I lay still for a whole minute waiting—nothing happened. What did he want? I wondered. Did he want to talk? If he did, our conversation would have been about nothing. He would ask me why I was there. I would lie and so would he. Or maybe we would have engaged in a talk about the law. That seemed to be the only intellectual discussion any of them could have, though a few would get excited and angry as they gave their input on how a statute should be interpreted and how their judges wrongly ruled on their case. Maybe he wanted me to pass a book or something to the next cell. If so, that might be a trap to lure me to the bars so he could throw a cup of shit in my face. Throwing styrofoam cups or milk cartons filled with body waste at each other was one of the many different fighting methods prisoners used at Camp J. At no time did any of us have contact with one another except through the bars of adjoining cells. We lived alone in individual cells and showered separately. It was because we never came in contact with each other that when they argued, they found other ways to fight. Fighting was called "going to war," and throwing feces was a favorite fighting tool.

I didn't store waste in my toilet like the rest of them did; I couldn't stand the smell. My neighbor knew I wasn't saving the weapon of choice because being next door to me, he could hear my toilet flush. So he knew that if he threw anything on me I had nothing to retaliate with. I wasn't taking any chances, so I didn't answer. I just wanted to do my time quietly, to hurry out of there.

The next day during lunch, that prisoner tried getting my attention again. When I pulled my tray into my cell, he started beating with his fist on the wall that separated us.

"Say!" he hollered, pounding on the wall. "I know you hear me over there."

I wish he would leave me alone, I thought. He kept beating on the wall.

"Say! I just want to tell you something," he said. "I ain't trying to kick no trouble with you."

I knew he wasn't going away. He knew I was awake, so I answered, "What?"

"I know you get bored over there, he said. "Here," and he held a tablet and pen out in front of my bars. "Write a letter to yourself or something; it helps pass the time."

"That's all right," I told him from the back of my cell, "I got enough to do."

"Say man, I'm trying to leave from back here too, so you don't have to worry about me. I'm only trying to help you, that's all."

I thought for a moment, then told him, "Drop the tablet in my cell."

He did, and I waited a couple of minutes before I went to pick it up. I sat on my bed and wrote:

I am eating lunch. Everyone on my tier is up. This is not good. When they are up, all of them start talking at the same time, and what they are saying is about nothing.

One prisoner yells out, "Nigga, I had money out in them streets. You the one ain't have nothing."

Another prisoner hollers, "You a hoe," to one of the other prisoners.

The prisoner two cells from me is in his cell air vent telling the prisoner in the cell behind him, "That bitch ratted on me," and I hear my other neighbor asking the prisoner picking up our trays, "How many stamps you want to bet on the game tonight?" I was glad when they went to sleep. I have never heard so much ignorance in one place.

After I wrote these few lines, I looked them over, then set the tablet on the floor and took a nap.

When I woke a few hours later the tier was quiet again. I lay in my bed thinking of nothing really when I picked up the tablet and wrote:

It is 5:30: I am sitting on my bed looking around at how bare my

29

cell is. Besides a metal toilet, a sink, and bunk there is nothing else. Stacked on the floor, I have two toilet paper rolls in the corner. The cell walls are painted white and the concrete floor has a jagged crack running the length of the cell. The bars of the cell are narrow and painted gray. Some places on the bars the gray paint is chipped off, revealing the red color they used to be painted. My cell has no air conditioner to cool me from the heat, and the heaters don't work. So I know in the summer this cell will be a hot box, just like the cold makes me feel like I'm sleeping in a freezer so I have to ball up under my blanket to stay warm at night.

"OK, that's it," I said, reading over my draft. As I wrote, I had thought about writing how Camp J was made up of four separate X shaped buildings. Each building was named after a fish: Gar, Shark, Gator, and Cuda. The prisoners who worked there bringing food to us lived in a dormitory named after a fish: Bass. Each side of the X wing was a tier, rows of twelve-man cells, thirteen if you counted the shower. In the center of each X was a central lobby. There guards sat drinking coffee, talking, and reading the newspaper, while they waited for their time to get off work.

If I had written anything about the physical structure of Camp J, I would have made sure to mention the small dog pens that were behind each building wing. That was where guards brought prisoners who wanted their rec time. Most prisoners, including me, never went out there because there was not enough room in those pens to do anything but stand in a spot and look crazy or holler out to the prisoner in another pen. But for those who did want to go out there, three times a week they were brought out of their cells in leg shackles, a waist chain, and handcuffs, and locked in one of the pens for fifteen minutes. Out there, the only thing the guard would take off them were the leg shackles so the prisoners could walk unhindered around in a small circle. That was another reason I never went out to the pens for rec: I didn't like the idea of staying chained up.

The physical structure of Camp J probably would have been OK to write about, but I only had a few sheets of paper left, so I thought better of it.

As I sat thinking of other things to write about, I heard a prisoner on the tier say, "You don't want to give me the short, motherfucker."

"I save all my shorts," a prisoner responded.

A short is the butt of a cigarette. At Camp J, no prisoners sent there for disciplinary punishment were allowed to smoke. But for $12 to $15 worth of stamps and a Dial soap, the prisoners that brought us our food trays would sell a 79¢ pack of Bugelar to whoever was willing to pay their steep price. 49¢ lighters cost an extra $7-8. Paying such high prices kept those prisoners who smoked from sharing with those prisoners who could not afford them. And since a smoker always had a craving, once the scent of nicotine was in the air, that prisoner's craving made him ask for the "short" of the cigarette. The response was always "No," which started the argument between prisoners.

"So you ain't gonna throw me the short?" the prisoner said.

"What I said."

"You ain't sending it?"

"No."

"Suit up, motherfucker."

I hated hearing those words "Suit up," because they meant that they were going to "War fight" by throwing piss mixed with shit at each other's cells. I hated for prisoners to fight like that because of the nauseating smell throwing waste produced on the tier. But what could I say? The first rule at Camp J was you never butt in another man's business.

"I'm suited up, motherfucker."

There were a few moments of silence, then I heard a milk carton filled with waste knock and splatter on the floor.

"Clean up bitch."

Another milk carton hit the floor.

"Now you clean up bitch."

Wiping up the waste that was in front of their cells required some maneuvering skills. You had to be able to move out of the way quickly as the next milk carton came while you cleaned up the mess in front of your cell. That day one of the prisoners was not successful in getting out of the way of the thrown milk carton; it dropped and splashed in his face.

"Got you bitch, got you bitch," one of the prisoners kept repeating.

"Got something for you," the prisoner responded, and with that statement I saw a small ball of fire bounce off the tier wall and roll in front of the other prisoner's cell. Then that prisoner took a small squirt bottle filled with lighter fluid and skeeted it at the ball of fire. Apparently that prisoner had a "shield" up; he had tied the four corners of his sheet to his cell bars to block any waste from splattering in his cell. So what the other prisoner was doing with the fire ball was attempting to "burn the prisoner out of the cell," by setting the sheet on fire. I could smell the smoke from the burning sheet.

"Don't you rat bitch, don't you rat," the prisoner who had thrown the fireball said. And as the other prisoner was trying to put out the fire and take down his sheet, he was hit with three or four milk cartons filled with shit. I shook my head.

Such a fight like those prisoners had would go on until they both were out of waste or it came close for a guard to come on the tier, which was only at shift time or to shower us. No prisoner who had a little "respect" about himself risked getting caught throwing shit. That was considered ratting. And if the guards caught you, they usually would move you to another tier. That was never a good thing. As with every area of the prison, word would be sent through the air vents that you "checked out," got the guards to remove you to avoid a fight. Such a rumor would then cause the prisoners on the tier you were moved on to team together to "run" you off the tier by throwing waste at you or "starve you out," paying the prisoners who carried food trays not to feed you. Those prisoners who brought the food down the tiers went along with everything a prisoner in those cells demanded; they didn't want to be shot with a dart or have anything thrown on them.

One of the strange rules kept among prisoners at J was that while two prisoners were fighting, everyone on the tier must be quiet. I thought the reason for the rule was so that we could hear the action and what the prisoners said to one another. Though that might have been a reason for the rule it was not the central reason. It was just a rule that has been passed along that everyone followed. Why? No one told me. Whatever the reason was I went along with it. So as those prisoners fought, I went to sleep.

I woke up a while later and the prisoners who had been fighting were now asleep. The tier was quiet again, quiet enough so that I could hear myself think. That was something I did a lot of in that cell. I would lie on my bed for hours thinking about my life, trying to determine where it all started to go wrong for me. I kept going back to that cursed number 16, my age when I got arrested. It was also the age at which my mother gave birth to me. I was the first baby born to a teenager in my family. My grandmother once told me that she felt like the 18 year old boy had taken advantage of her baby girl. But she never really forgave my mother for getting pregnant. I don't believe her older siblings did, either.

My grandmother was a very dictatorial woman. While my grandfather was a quiet, hardworking man, my grandmother was the voice for the family. She raised her children with a stiff belt. She boasted that she and my grandfather were looked at among the Eden Garden Community as upstanding citizens who attended church every Sunday and who were raising decent, respectful children. My mother told me that when she or one of her brothers or sisters were any place, my grandmother demanded their best behavior or they would be greeted with a belt when they got home. Everyone knew the Harper children, my mother said, so when she became pregnant, my grandmother felt my mother had brought a dark cloud over the family. Through her words, the family ostracized my mother, treated her like a disease that had affected "the family" body that they wished they could get rid of but couldn't. So they suffered with my mother. I was seen by them as the source of their suffering, and the agony of looking at me became so unbearable at times that my grandmother would narrow her black eyes at me, tighten her lips, and in the harshest tone she could manage, say, "You not no Harper! Don't you ever forget that 'cause I don't ever want to hear you say you're one of us 'cause you're not." I can still recall after my mother moved us out of my grandparents' home, that whenever we went back to visit, my grandmother wouldn't allow me inside her home. I had to stay in the back yard. At six or seven I didn't perceive that as rejection but as I got older, I began to notice how my grandmother would let her other grandchildren go freely in and out of the house, but not me. If I wanted a drink of water, I had to request it at the side door and one of my cousins would go in for it. Most times, however, to avoid being teased by my cousins, I drank from the backyard water hose.

Such treatment by my grandmother along with her always reminding me I was not to be considered part of "her" family, slowly beat me down to an emotional numbness so that by the time I was fourteen, I did not see myself as part of the family. So I reasoned that I didn't have to listen to any of them, and I didn't.

And that attitude was partially why I was in that cell. No one could tell me anything. I never compromised. I lay there in my bed and thought about that, but I reasoned with myself that I wasn't born with that attitude. The way I grew up, I needed it to survive. "And they put me in prison," I said to myself, "when they don't even know my circumstances." I began having mixed feelings of anger, to sadness, to anger again. I remember looking down at the tablet on the floor and thinking I should write about my life and call it The Making of a Criminal. I picked up the pen and tablet and wrote:

The Life of Fabian Harper

Shortly after my mother gave birth to me she moved us in with Billy Ray George, a man she eventually married. I was probably only 6, but I can still remember how angry my mother's marriage made my grandmother. She used to tell my mother to let me spend weekends with her; however, the purpose of those sleepovers was not for family bonding. Those nights I spent with my grandmother were interrogation sessions. For hours, she would make me stand in front of her as she asked me question after question about my mother and Billy, hoping to uncover some sinister secret that she believed I knew. Of course I didn't know any secrets, I was too young. But that didn't stop my grandmother from questioning me.

When the weekend was over, my mother would meet my grandmother with the other family members at the family church, Paradise Baptist Church, and after the service take me home with her. In the car, my mother would put me through another series of questioning. She would ask what I did at grandmother's and what we all talked about. I told my mother everything. She had drilled in me to always be honest with her. Even today, I share with her everything about my life, even if I know she will get upset. Sometimes she does, just like when I was a child riding home from church beside her in that car. If I had told my grandmother something that she thought I shouldn't have, I got scolded. "What goes on in our house stays in our house. You don't tell nobody, not even your grandmother," she would lecture to me. Being a child of 6 or 7 years old, what my mother had told me didn't make sense. She had taught me to be honest, to always tell the truth. And if I loved my family and wanted to be loved, I would never lie to them. But she was telling me to lie to my grandmother. I didn't understand why, and many times I felt confused and afraid because I did not want to lose either my mother's or grandmother's love. But my mother's sharp words, "Just do as I say," forced me to choose. And every time my grandmother asked me a question, I lied. Most times I didn't really feel like I was lying to my grandmother, because a lot of the questions I really did not know the answer to. But when she would ask me about Billy... well, I knew I was lying.

Billy was an alcoholic, I knew that. Growing up in his house I saw him drink a lot and wanted to imitate him. I adored my stepfather. I would watch him drink his can of beer, and after he would go to sleep, I would tiptoe into the room where he was, grab the empty beer can and drink the little amount of beer at the bottom of the can. One time he caught me. He woke up to see me lifting the can to my tiny mouth. I was terrified when his bloodshot eyes opened to stare into mine as he took the can. I thought for sure he would be upset with me, but he wasn't. Instead, he reached down into a paper sack on the floor next to his bed, pulled from it another can of beer, popped the top to down three fourths of it, then handed me the rest to drink. I was eight years old. His reasoning for giving me that can of beer was simple: "I'd rather see you drink at home with me than out in the street where you can get into trouble," he told me. That was how I started drinking. The only good thing I can say about that experience is I never grew up to become an alcoholic like he was.

Over the next few years that my mother was married to Billy, I watched him vomit repeatedly, only to pass out later on the floor or living room sofa. Many nights I awoke to the noise he made staggering into the house from being out late drinking, and stumbling down the hall knocking pictures off the wall on his way to bed. As his drinking got worse, so did his temper with my mother.

Billy would come home and start fussing at my mother about nothing. One afternoon he tried to hit her, but she quickly put a stop to him. He had come in late, drunk, and asked my mother why she hadn't cooked. She had, and she told him that because it seemed to her that he wouldn't be home until late, she had put his food in the refrigerator. He didn't like her answer and they started arguing. Their voices kept getting louder and louder, one trying to talk over the other, when Billy's anger erupted and he slapped my mother across her cheek. "Ah!" I heard my mother exclaim; then there was silence, and I saw Billy walk past my bedroom door headed for their room where he went in and passed out. My mother waited until she was sure he was asleep, then pulled his 38 pistol from his drawer. She pressed the barrel against his temple and pulled the trigger. Luckily, the gun wasn't loaded. I don't know what woke him, the click of the gun's hammer striking the firing pin, maybe the gun barrel's cold steel on his skin. But whatever it was, his eyes stared into the black hole of that barrel that my mother had now pointed between his eyebrows. After that, my mother never had to worry about him hitting her again. That incident may have stopped Billy from becoming physically abusive, but it did little to stop their arguing.

Many nights I stayed awake in my bed staring at the ceiling, listening to my mother's and Billy's yelling voices coming through my bedroom wall. I prayed to God that they would stop arguing, but He never answered my prayer. They fussed about money, about Billy's drinking, and about him forgetting to pay a bill. I can remember times coming home from school and walking into a cold, dark house because Billy forgot to pay the gas or light bill. Actually, he hadn't forgot but used the money to get drunk. This became routine practice for him every bill day. Billy had neglected everything but his drinking. He neglected his hygiene, even eating. He drank so much that he started having alcoholic seizures. I will never forget the first seizure he had one Sunday morning at home.

Like every Sunday morning, my mother was in the kitchen cooking breakfast. She had turned the stereo all the way up in the living room so she could hear her two favorite Christian radio preachers, Frederick Price and Reverend Ike. I still remember "Paradise," Frederick Price's theme song and Reverend Ike saying, "You can write me, Reverend Ike, at General Post Office Box 50, New York, New York, or you can call me at 1-800-453-9000." Billy was in their bedroom trying to sleep off a hangover.

When she finished preparing breakfast, she came into my room and woke me. I used to get up excited about Sunday breakfast. I used to call it that because that's when I ate a full morning meal. Other mornings I was fed a bowl of cereal. Bananas in Cheerio's was my favorite. But that Sunday morning my mother had fixed yellow scrambled eggs, crisp fried bacon, and white grits. I sat at the table gobbling down my meal while my mother called for Billy to come into the kitchen and eat. He came, but was in no mood to eat.

"You know I got a headache!" he yelled at my mother as he came through the doorway. "And why you got the stereo up?"

"Billy, sit down and eat," my mother said.

"I don't want to eat. I want you to shut up and turn the stereo down," and at that statement, they started arguing.

While they argued, I hurried to eat my food so I could leave because I did not want to hear them fussing at each other.

I went to my room to dress for church. I had a suit that I loved to wear—a gray double-breasted suit with a shiny polyester dark gray collar. As I pulled the suit from the closet, I could still hear my mother's and Billy's voices.

Taking off my PJ's, I stood looking in my dresser mirror, matching shirts with the suit jacket, when I heard my mother holler, "Billy!" I paused for a moment, then went right back to looking in the mirror.

"Billy!" I heard my mother holler again. "Billy, what's wrong with you?"

Pots fell to the floor and plates broke. "Billy! Where are..." —then I saw him run past my door into their bedroom. My mother chased after him. "Billy, Billy!"

I dropped my clothes and ran behind my mother into their room and saw Billy on the floor shaking violently.

"Quick," my mother told me, "go next door and get help."

I ran in my Spider Man undies as fast as I could next door to my friend Vondray's dad. They were just getting into the car for church.

If I had to point at where the downward spiral of my life started, I would say it was Billy's Sunday morning seizure. After it, my life was one collapse after collapse.

Billy had other seizures at home, on his drinking corner, and at work. That was when his job referred him to treatment. He had to successfully complete a 90-day alcoholic program or they would fire him.

He accepted being admitted.

My mother and I had to attend rehab meetings with him. I hated to go to those therapy sessions. We were supposed to be there for support, and though I enjoyed the moments I spent with him in his room playing Monopoly and Pitty Pat, we were the only black family there. When all the families came in together in the evening for group discussion, we were always the ones asked all the questions. The group leader made me feel like it was my mom's and my fault that Billy drank. It was like we were there in treatment, not him. That's why it wasn't a shock to me when he relapsed hours after his release from the hospital.

It wasn't long after Billy completed his therapy that my mother became pregnant with my sister. Billy was against having more children. Since he was helping my mother take care of me and he had two children to provide for from a previous marriage, another child only increased the financial stress he was under, he told my mother. So when he found out that my mother was pregnant, he was livid. They argued and fussed more. Not long after Marquita was born, my mother left Billy.

She kept me home from school that one day. When Billy left for work, my grandfather came from around the corner in a U-Haul truck. My grandfather and my mother's brother loaded everything in the house into that truck, leaving behind only the crimson red living room carpet and kitchen stove. I imagined Billy's shock when he walked into that empty house after work.

I cried for days when I found out I wasn't going back home to Billy. I blamed myself for my mother leaving him, since some of their arguments were about me. I can remember going to my mother, apologizing for whatever I had done, and begging her to go back to Billy. She told me "No!" and to leave her alone about him. For a long time I was mad at my mother for divorcing Billy. He was the only man I ever felt cared about me. He was an alcoholic, but at least he wasn't like the man who impregnated my mother with me. That man, besides lying down with my mother, had nothing to do with me. I knew who he was. At times we walked right past each other on the sidewalk with no gesture, no polite wave to each other. One time my mother took me to his mother for a visit and he was there. When he heard that I was in the front room, he ran out the back door just to avoid speaking to me, as if I was a police officer coming to arrest him. But Billy was different. He paid attention to me. He took time out to talk to me, to make me feel like I was his child. Even after the divorce we stayed in touch. He used to call from the Fina gas station, the corner where he spent his days drinking, his "office," and I could call there at any time I wanted to talk to him. Later, he died from cirrhosis of the liver due to alcohol. After that I was alone.

After my mother left Billy, she found a rent house to move us into, in a poor, dangerous part of the city. She had to get three jobs to support my sister and me. That time was hard for our little family. I helped by staying home to babysit my little sister whenever my mother went to work. There was seldom enough to feed the three of us. Often my mother would have only enough money to buy milk formula for my sister. Some nights I pretended not to be hungry so she wouldn't have to buy more food to feed me. I used to sneak across the fence that divided us from our neighbor's yard at night and steal buckets of water from their outdoor water hydrant so we could bathe. I collected Coke bottles and cans to sell for extra money. But there was never enough. No one from my mother's family would lift a finger to help us. Either they didn't know what was going on or didn't care, probably the latter, knowing them. For a long time all my mother, Marquita and I had were each other and a shoddy house to protect us from the outdoor cold and heat, nothing more. We slept on the floor. There was no gas, no lights, no nothing.

We were at our lowest as a family when my mother met this truck driver, Edward Davis. She brought him home to meet my sister and me. I looked at him and hated him. I knew he was nothing, and wondered why she found him desirable. He was a liar, a cheat, and besides driving trucks, he sold drugs and used them. I can see the two of us, me and him, me and this man, seated across from each other staring eye to eye while he tried to make friendly conversation with me in our living room. One day my mother walked in to tell me that they were getting married. My eyes widened, stunned by the announcement.

My shock quickly turned to anger, and I asked her why she had to marry him.

"Because I love him, " she said.

"You just met this guy!" I shot back. "How can you love him?"

"I'm the grown-up," she snapped. "You don't question me." Then she snatched up her purse from the sofa and walked out the door with Edward, leaving me to watch my sister.

They walked back through the door an hour later laughing, hugging, and kissing. He had taken her to the nearest justice of the peace. There was no honeymoon.

After the marriage, Edward left for the road. He stayed gone for months before my mother heard from him, and that was by phone. He called to let her know that he was in town but he couldn't come home right then because he had to stay with his truck while it went through inspection. My mother believed him. When she finally did see him, about two days later, she asked for money to pay a bill. He didn't have any money, he told her, and gave her the sorriest excuse for why he was broke. "My job froze all our checks," he said. But he promised that as soon as they released his checks, his job would send them to her. It was almost the same excuse every time she saw him for why he didn't have any money to give her, or it would be he had to get his truck fixed, or the gas was way higher upstate, just one lame excuse after another. I knew he wasn't ever going to give my mother any money, but she kept believing in him, why I don't know.

One time Edward's pay check was mailed to my mother. $2050, and she thought her prayers were finally answered, that Edward had finally come around. It was later she learned his job had accidentally sent the check to her, but not before she cashed that check, paid a few bills, bought some food for us, and treated herself to some minor luxuries.

When Edward came home looking for his check, they argued. Edward yelled at her that she was going to pay him back every penny; then he left, slamming the door. He wasn't heard from for months. I was glad, but I didn't know he was burning up my mother's credit card, buying things when he was on the road: food, gas, a TV. My mother soon had to file bankruptcy due to the debt he had put her in.

Since Edward wasn't giving my mother any money, she had to continue working the three jobs. Every day and night she worked, only coming home for a few hours to eat and take short naps. I recall going into her room one day, asking her why she didn't leave Edward the way she had left Billy. She told me to get out.

Though my mother held out hope that Edward would change, I didn't. Seeing how worn out she would be after coming in from work, dropping flat on her face in bed, not bothering to take off her shoes or clothes, I no longer held on to her optimism for a better life that she thought marrying Edward would bring. Recalling those times, I can hear her words. "Just have faith," she'd say. "God gonna see us through." Then she would tell me to go read my Bible. After an hour I would return to her room and sit on the floor next to her bed and tell her "thus said the Lord." I tried desperately to believe in His words myself.

Things only got worse for us. I tried to pitch in and help as much as I could. Keeping the lawn cut and hedges trimmed, I learned how to cook, wash and iron clothes, clean dishes, keet the house dusted and vacuumed, and watch my sister. I didn't have time to play with kids my age. I was the man of the house, my mother told me, and had to act like one, so playing with other kids was out.

I grew up quick.

The stress of our little family's bleak circumstances got to my mother. Her long black hair fell out in clumps. She stopped going to church, stopped caring about her appearance, and the little attention that she gave me and Marquita, she stopped that. Sleep and work was all she did. As her aggravation grew, so did her frustration with me. She started whipping me. She whipped me for the slightest things. No matter how hard I tried to help, I stayed doing something wrong in her eyes. I eventually got tired of getting hit for nothing and ran away, only to return a few nights later to be whipped for leaving. That night, I decided to stand there and take my lashes like a man. I wasn't going to cry, I told myself. It didn't matter how long she whipped me or how hard she hit me; I had made up my mind that I was not going to cry and scream any more. That night would be a test of wills, and I was determined to prove my point that my will was greater than her belt lashes. Over time, I began to see the whippings mother gave me as a sign that she hated me. I developed a hostile attitude toward everything, including her.

I was only 11 or 12, but watching my exhausted mother come home every day fueled the hatred I felt toward Edward. I saw him as the source of my mother's anguish, the reason for my whippings, and I wanted to get back at him for all the grief he had caused. I wanted him to feel pain.

I had my chance to do that when he came home for a weekend. Edward was sitting at the kitchen table playing dominoes with my cousin Adrian; I was lying across my mother's bed watching her TV. Edward could see the picture from where he sat, and when I flipped the channel without asking him, he told me to turn the station back. I ignored him. When he saw that I wasn't going to change it, he went to the television and turned it back to the program he was watching. I had the remote and turned the television to another channel. Seeing this, he walked over to me to grab the remote, but I hit him in the face with it, and while he was dazed, I managed to get a few licks with my fist in

41

his face. If it weren't for my mother getting in front of him, I would have kept beating him.

Right after this fight with Edward, my grades started to drop at school. Before, I had excelled in subjects I liked and was average in those that didn't interest me. Sometimes I studied for a test, but I hardly turned in homework, yet I still managed to pull out C averages by the end of nine weeks.. But with the troubles at home, I stopped caring about school. My report card became a row of F's. The only class that I wasn't failing was English. Because I had no voice at home, English class was my place of refuge. There I could demand the attention of my teacher and peers without interruption, express myself without fear, and expect to be heard. I felt secure in my world of words, where I could control the outcome. With English, I was able to escape to a new life that I would live out through paper and ink.

It was my sixth grade teacher at Ridgewood Middle School, Mrs. Jaubert, who first discovered my interest in writing. I recall she had the class reading aloud a story from a literature book. I was at my desk writing one of my own, when she called on me to read.

"Fabian, start where Michael stopped."

I looked down at the book page, my eyes searching for the spot to begin as I tried to remember the last words Michael read.

"You don't know where we are, do you?" she asked.

"No, Ma'am."

"What are you doing that you can't pay attention to class?" She rose from her wood chair and began her walk toward me. At my desk she picked up the sheet of paper I had been writing on, and started reading it aloud. I guess she thought that I was writing a love note to a girl, as most young boys occupied their time doing at that age, and wanted to embarrass me. But I was writing a story about Halloween. Mid-way into the second paragraph she stopped reading, gave me back my paper, and told me to see her after class.

When we met, Mrs. Jaubert said, "You have a very active imagination," and told me for extra credit she would give me home assignments different from the class. My first lesson was to write a story about my summer. I didn't realize it then, but that was Mrs. Jaubert's way of nurturing my writing. When I didn't do the assignment, she looked at me with straight lips and said, "You could have been someone special." Mrs. Jaubert gave up on me that day. If she had bothered to ask, she would have learned that I had long ago given up on myself.

Because my grades were not improving, the assistant principal, Mr. Lynn, called my mother to come to his office. I sat beside her listening to Mr. Lynn tell her why I would be repeating the sixth grade. Besides poor grades, I had a behavior problem, he told my mother. This so angered her that she told him she would be transferring me to another school. She believed that because Ridgewood was predominantly white, Mr. Lynn had reason to see me as a problem. Looking back, I see that the real problem was my acting out due to neglect.

That summer my mother signed me up to sing with the neighborhood gospel group, the Bright Star Male Chorus. It was in the choir that I met V.C., a gay fifteen year old. I was placed in a small section between high-pitched singers and those with middle range voices. V.C. stood right next to me. Since I was new to the group, I didn't know a lot of the songs and would ask him the words. V.C. quickly fell in love with me. He would mischievously cut his brown eyes at me as we sang. His distant expression whenever some other man in the group approached me, his careful way of speaking in conversation, as well as the special attention he paid me whenever we went on singing engagements— all revealed his deep interest in me.

During my years with the choir, V.C. and I were inseparable. We stayed in the same hotel rooms and never took our eyes off each other when we went out of town with the choir. I went with him to the gay teen clubs, and we even slept weekend nights at each other's homes. I enjoyed my time with V.C. He entered my life at a time when I had no continuity at home. He treated me as though I was someone special, a person of value. And he always listened to the things I had to say; even if he disagreed, he listened still. I knew with him I mattered. People who knew us would call us brothers—and that was the way we acted.

That summer I was able to laugh with V.C., but my joy ended when right before school was about to start my mother told me I wouldn't be getting any school supplies. "I can't provide for you any longer," she told me. "You got to get a job to take care of yourself." Her words didn't come as a total shock; I had expected them. In fact, I had been waiting for her to tell me I had to find someplace else to live, but she didn't put me out. But I did have to get a job. As I write, I can still see the hurt in my mother's eyes that day. They were weary. I remember her saying I was her only son, her special child, and I could accomplish anything I put my mind to, and how I was going to be somebody special. "I just know it," she told me, tears in her eyes. Whether she said that for her own encouragement I don't know, but her words I have always carried with me, and they have pushed me to never stop trying.

I stood looking at her, wondering who would hire a 12 year old child. My mother said that she could get me a job working at her third job, a janitorial service, cleaning office buildings at night. They won't ask your age," she said. "Having the building clean is all they care about."

The next day, I had to go to the janitorial main office and sign a contract before beginning the job. When I walked into the small, smoke-filled room, I was met by a tall and very large man. He was middle-aged, his big round belly sagged over his belt and he chomped down on a unlit cigar that hung from the corner of his mouth. He glared down at me and pulling the fat cigar out of his mouth, asked, "Can you handle a buffer?"

"Yessir." My voice cracked a little.

He stared at me . I stood there paralyzed by fear, due to what I did not know. Maybe it was his deep voice or the way he chewed on his cigar, leaving pieces of brown tobacco stuck between his teeth. Maybe it was the way he wore his black hair slicked back on his head that reminded me of a mob boss named Vinny, or maybe it was the simple way he said his name—Jack. He told me the rules of the job.

"You work three hours a night from seven 'til ten," he said. "I won't pay you for more, and you don't get paid if the job is not complete. I want the floors buffed, trash cans dumped, toilets cleaned, and furniture dusted. If you get sick or can't make it to work, call me. But you better have a good reason why you can't make it or I will fire you. Got it?"

"Yessir."

"I see you're kinda young, but your momma said you needed the work. He pointed his cigar at me: "You don't ask nobody nothing, you don't tell nobody nothing, you just clean, got it?"

"Yessir."

He stopped talking and stood there studying me. I stood still, almost holding my breath. After a few moments of silent contemplation, he stuck the cigar back into his mouth and said, "You can go."

I went to work that night at the office building of Lennex-Heathcraft Corporation, their copper and tube division. My first duty of the night was to buff the floor. I wanted to get the hardest part of the job out of the way. I stripped the floor of all its old wax, then buffed new wax into the brown marble floor. When I first turned the buffer on, it took off, hit a desk, bounced off a wall, and rammed straight into a floor flower pot before I managed to turn it off. I remember my mother telling me to put the handle under my navel and lean forward a little. After a few tries, I finally was able to guide it. Soon I was so good I could control that buffer with only one hand and my waist.

When my shift was over, V.C. came to pick me up. I was happy to see him every time he drove up. After spending the night dumping trash cans, cleaning toilets, and buffing floors, I would be exhausted. V.C. always had something for me to eat when he came. Some nights he took me straight home, but most nights I slept at his mother's house. It wasn't a big deal that I didn't come home. My mother didn't need me there. Since I was working, my grandmother watched my sister, and my mother would be at work or asleep, so there was no reason for her to miss me.

I worked all that summer with no problem, but when the school year started, I faced a new set of challenges. I attended Midway Middle School, one of the roughest junior high schools in the city. The students were mostly black, with about a dozen or so whites bussed there for integration purposes. Midway students' attitude toward school was different than the white students' at Ridgewood.

At Ridgewood, academics were stressed, and the children there held high self esteem for making good grades. At Midway, however, kids took pride in one thing—who could fight the best. Naturally being a child at a new school, I wanted to fit in. If I wanted to be popular at Midway, that road would be won by bloody battles, and not with my brain.

Fights were arranged by a simple method. The only thing that was required was for one to be challenged to a fight in front of other students. This was usually done when students changed classes when everybody would be in the halls. If you didn't accept the challenge, you were marked a coward and ended up fighting nearly everyone in the school because they were going to pick on you. Even teachers were sucked into this, calling some kids cowards because they had refused to fight. The fights took place after school. There would be as many as five or six fights scheduled. The fights took place across the street from the school in a small grass field on a tiny dirt mound that students called Boot Hill. That field would be packed with kids watching other kids square off against each other on that mound. Kids would be hollering, yelling, and jumping up and down for their champion to win. I witnessed some brutal fights on that mound. School administrators occasionally drove by to observe a fight. Some even parked their cars and watched kids beat each other. The first couple of times I saw school teachers smiling while watching the fights, I wondered why they never tried to break any of them up. But after a while, I stopped thinking about it.

My first fight on that mound happened when a kid stood in the school hall between classes and hollered out to me, "Say! Meet me on the hill after school."

I was standing in front of my social studies class door. My heart started beating faster, tiny beads of sweat came on my arms and forehead, but with a hall full of other kids looking at me, I shouted back, "Nigga, you ain't nothing! You just make sure you're there, that's all!"

That afternoon after school, I was on the mound ready to do battle for my "respect." In front of me was a boy who looked like he should have been in the tenth or eleventh grade, but instead he was still at Midway, stuck in the seventh grade, and facing me. "What you want to do?" he asked, stretching his arms wide like he was about to be nailed to a cross.

Every fighter asked this question before any punches were thrown, hoping to get an easy victory. The one who backed down would be ridiculed and marked as a coward. No one wanted to be labeled a coward. And standing on that mound, I knew that if I wanted respect at school, wanted to be popular, there was only one way to answer the boy's question.

"You called me out here," I snarled at him, "so you must got something on your mind you need me to get off for you."

With a crowd of kids looking on we exchanged a few more words, then simultaneously charged each other. Since he had a stocky body, he tried to wrestle me to the ground. But being narrow, I was more agile than he was, so I could throw a fast punch, then move quickly out of his striking range. The fight lasted for all of about two minutes. We were both tired after that. I didn't win that fight, but I didn't lose it either. After the fight, the kids that had stood watching us told me that I had done OK, but I could have been better. The problem, I learned, was that I didn't have a fighting style. Style made the difference between being congratulated when you won or praised if you looked good while winning. I wanted to be praised.

I went home and started practicing my fighting technique, throwing punches, working on my stance, and moving swiftly. Soon I was looking good winning fights. My name became the talk of the school, and I started calling boys out to meet me on Boot Hill. I was finally becoming liked. I loved this. Looking back, I know that engaging myself in such a barbaric tradition further undermined my development and subjected me to seeking the gratification of my peers through violence.

With no attention at home, I sought the praise of the kids around me. And their accolades were like a drug. You want more of it. After a while, you get caught in this cycle where it is "expected" by other kids to act a certain way. You want to stop, but it's hard.

With fight wins came popularity, and also trouble. I quickly developed enemies, boys who didn't appreciate my fame. These boys came together and beat me to a bloody mess. I still have a deep scar over my left eyebrow from that assault. I had neglected to do one thing as I earned my status, to form alliances with other boys who were also popular. Since it was too late to be popular with that group of boys, I teamed instead with a less popular boy who could fight. C. L. Banks was light skinned, almost white, with long, curly black hair. Girls adored C.L. and this was the cause of most of his fights. We started hanging out together, watching each other's back and fighting together.

Midway's poor academic standards and school violence eventually got the attention of the School Board Administrators, and they sent someone to rid the school of its bad reputation. They sent Mr. Lynn, my assistant principal from Ridgewood. I saw him and thought, What bad luck. Mr. Lynn's first order of business was to call me into his office for a talk.

"I see you have made a name for yourself here, Fabian," I remember him saying. I just looked at him. "Well, I'm here now and I'm not going to let you run my school, understood?"

I didn't say anything.

"Another thing," he continued, "you and your friend C.L.. are not to be together. I don't want to see him around you in this school. If I do, I will put you, not him, in detention or in school suspension class, you understand me?"

I gave him a despising glance.

"Another thing," he said, "I don't want to hear of your fighting again." That stunned me . Not letting me hang out with my only friend C.L. at school was one thing, but trying to control my life after school—that was something different. I spoke up.

"But what if somebody messes with me first?" I asked, my voice at a high pitch.

"You better walk away," he said. "If you don't, I will kick your butt out of this school."

"Walk away!" Did he really know what he was saying? To walk away from a challenge was to risk being seen as a coward. To walk away was to abandon the thing that gave me identity, a voice that was heard. I had created a name that gave me acceptance into a society that I would not otherwise have easily passed through, my neighborhood. The blood I shed of others bought me admiration and prestige, and protection for my young sister when she played in the streets. Mr. Lynn saw me only as a problem, but in my world I was glorified, a leader. I held influence over the young kids and was respected by old people. Amid the anger, stress, and frustration that I woke up under every day, fighting gave me a credibility and privilege in the streets where I could provide for me and my family a few extra material things. To walk away?

It was easy for Mr. Lynn to sit across from me in his office that day and utter those words. But it was a lot more complicated than he understood. He was a white man who stayed miles away from the inner city where I lived. He saw the fighting, but he couldn't see the cause for the fighting. If he could have diagnosed that, he could have saved me.

I kept fighting and Mr. Lynn suspended me from school. Three days the first time, a week the second. I recall him saying, "I can't get through to you," and suggesting he should talk to my mother. Most students would have dreaded the principal calling their parents, but not me. I didn't care. My mother was too busy working and worrying about Edward to be concerned with me. She did not even know that I had been suspended twice from school. But after she talked to Mr. Lynn, she took me home and whipped me. As with all of my other whippings, I behaved for a few days until the pain had become a distant memory; then I was right back getting into trouble at school.

The attention I had received from kids spoiled me. As long as I was being praised by them, thinking that I was the "big attraction," I could continue to endure the lashes from my mother's belt. My behavior, though, was a masquerade. Soon, I could not break from the image I had created to reveal my true self. I was offered nothing to motivate me to change. My environment gave me nothing I could look forward to. To change just for the sake of changing was nothing, I thought. And I didn't want to be nothing. At least with the fighting and acting wild in class, I was an idol that everyone looked up to. I did the things that others weren't brave enough to do, and I relished being their hero.

My wild behavior soon won an audience at a rival school , J.S. Clark, and slowly my name drifted into conversations in neighborhoods across the city. I had entered into an arena I knew nothing about, and like a beginner swimmer who dives into deep water, I found myself in serious trouble.

One afternoon I stood on the school's steps waiting to be picked up by V.C. when I was approached by a guy asking for the time. When I looked down at my wrist, he punched me. Dazed, stumbling backwards, I managed to throw a couple of punches but they landed in the air. What saved me from a severe beating that day was a girl who walked out the front door of the school and started screaming. Her hollering ran the guy away. I still have a deep scar inside my lip from that attack.

The next day at school, in the halls were murmurs about what had happened to me. What type of revenge would I execute, kids wondered. Would I let the attacker get away? A lot rode on my decision. To not do anything jeopardized my respect, the only thing that made me feel I was somebody. I had to live up to my image. That attack only increased the spin of my life that had begun spiraling slowly out of control when my mother left Billy.

After C.L. and I talked about what happened, he decided we should go after the guy with a gun. This was an important step that we were about to take because no kids our age had ever thought about using a gun to settle a score; we always fist fought. In discussing our plot, the ramifications of using a gun on someone never entered our minds. We never considered, "What if we kill the guy?" All we wanted to do was get even in the worst way possible, to make him pay for what he had done. It wasn't that C.L. and I were heartless thugs, but our minds didn't gauge consequences. All we saw was our "revenge," and the statement that would be made by it. This gave us an excited rush, and wanting to continue that adrenaline flow gave us motivation.

After purchasing a gun from a neighborhood drug dealer, we planned to sneak onto the school bus that went to the guy's neighborhood where we would confront him. But our plan never made it to the end of the school day. C.L. got caught with the gun at school. To save himself from further trouble, he told Mr. Lynn that the gun belonged to me and what I had intended doing with it.

Mr. Lynn called me to his office and as soon as I walked in, I saw C.L. sitting in a chair with his head down. Then I looked on Mr. Lynn's desk and saw the gun.

"This yours?" he asked me, picking the gun up.

I didn't say anything.

He sat the gun back down on his desk, stood up, and walked over to me. I was still standing next to his door.

"Go sit down," he said, then closed the door behind me. I sat next to C.L.

"Look, C.L. told me everything," Mr. Lynn said. "Now you want to tell me your version?"

I cut my eyes at C.L., but he kept his head down. He couldn't even look at me. The code of the street was you didn't snitch on anybody, no matter the circumstances. Not even if it was your enemy. If you got accused wrongly, you had to accept it, to take your ride. That was just part of the code of street life.

Walking from the door, Mr. Lynn sat on the corner of his desk, and stared at me for a long moment. I stared back at him with a defiant glare. It was like we were playing the stare-down game that children play. Then he broke.

"You know, Fabian, you will be expelled from school if you let C.L. say this gun is yours."

I just looked at him.

"You don't want to save yourself?" he asked. "You want to be put out of school?"

I looked away at the wall.

"Fine. If that's how you want it. I..." and before he could finish his sentence, into his office walked a blue suited police officer.

"You called, sir?" he asked Mr. Lynn.

"Yes." Mr. Lynn stood to his feet and smiling, shook the officers' hand and said while picking the gun up, "This gun here was found at this school." He handed the gun to the officer, then pointed at me. "It belongs to him."

The officer slid the gun into his back pocket and pulled a set of handcuffs from his belt, then told me to stand and put my hands behind my back. After handcuffing me, the officer grabbed hold of my arm. Classes were changing when he led me out of Mr. Lynn's office past students standing in the hallway. He walked me to his car. Students watched from windows as he opened the car's back door, then put his hand on top of my head, guiding it down to the seat. This was my first arrest.

Two things ended with my arrest and expulsion from Midway Middle School: my friendship with C.L. and my mother's concern for me. Her preoccupation with Edward consumed any tenderness that she might have wanted to show toward me. She often told me that Marquita and I were more important than him, but her actions were what I paid attention to. Without her emotional support, I stopped caring how my life turned out. Her care for Edward angered me, especially since he only came by to eat, sleep, and store his drugs. One day my mother discovered that he was sleeping with another woman across town. Her life caved in completely after that.

After my arrest, I was expelled from Midway. I had to enroll in a School Away from School program that the Shreveport School System offered to students who were behavior problems at regular schools. The program was designed to put problematic students in a restricted class setting; all we did in that class was work, with no socializing with other students until after school. I had my own cubicle and was monitored by a teacher all day.

Most of the students there already knew who I was. The students came from the roughest neighborhoods in the city—Motown, Cedar

Grove, Hollywood, Lakeside, Allendale, Queensborough, Cooper Road— and we all fought against each other. At School Away I became acquainted with a group calling itself the Hollywood Grape Street Crip gang. I had already turned down the invitation to join the 19 Gang of Cedar Grove, the neighborhood where I was from, and the 60 Crip gang of Motown, the area where my mother had moved us to. But the Grape Street Crips intrigued me. Though only teenagers, they were not a bunch of loose kids running around. They were well-organized and close, like a family. This attracted me, and I began to hang around them after school.

Every day I would loiter with those boys outside an arcade store in Hollywood that was run by an older man who was also a Grape Crip member. Because of his age, 40, he had earned the noble status of O.G., short for Original Gangsters. This designation in gang culture was conferred on men and women who served the gang tirelessly for many years, displaying complete loyalty to the gang family. Like faithful church members who seek their elders' counsel, we sought advice and instruction from the O.G.'s. It wasn't long before the O.G.'s asked me to be a member of the Grape Street Crips. I accepted.

I had to pass two initiation processes. The first was standing within a circle of gang members and fighting all of them at one time. This ritual was called, "getting jumped into the gang," which was meant to instill the instinct to fight with everything in you for your survival and to show the compassion of your soon-to-be brothers, since they didn't kill you. The second phase of initiation was a six-month probation, during which I was tested to see whether I had ability to think under pressure, to show no mercy to the "family's" adversaries, and to bring useful skills to the family's business. The O.G.'s managed the drug trade business for Grape Street Crips on Fuller Street. Each street gang in the city had turf where they sold drugs. And it was part of a young member's job to help protect the neighborhood from intruders that tried to muscle their way into the gang's market.

The ranks of Grape Street from the top to the bottom was ordered, beginning with the eldest O.G. that oversaw the entire organization. Other O.G.'s were managers, third commanders who controlled distribution and coordinated different sections (street blocks) throughout the neighborhood, security personnel who provided protection to those who sold drugs to passing cars and people walking by.

I started as a peon. We "put in work" for the gang by engaging in gun battles with rival gangs to protect the "set," another name for street blocks where drugs were sold. I went on rides to take down any competition. Though getting shot at was dangerous, going on rides used to scare me the most. Like a military general commanding his unit of young soldiers, the O.G. would direct us to go out alone to hit the different drug dealers on their turf. Besides going out on rides, I used to walk up to one of the workers and, after asking to buy $50 worth of drugs, snatch the tiny bags of cocaine from his hand and run off. After doing that a few times, I realized that snatching small bags of drugs really wasn't hampering their sales, so I started going up to groups of men on corners and taking their drug money and jewelry at gun point.

I put in this sort of work for my gang family all summer. The money that I took in those hustles I was allowed to keep, but the drugs went to the gang, and we shared in the profits. I was collecting enough money to quit my janitorial job but was told by an O.G. not to. Anyone who made untaxed money in the street needed a disguise, he told me, and having a job served as the perfect front.

I wasted my extra money on clothes. The highest style in the late eighties was a silk shirt, Levi jeans, a baseball cap, and python cowboy boots or Ropers. But instead of the boots I purchased a lot of sneakers that I changed out of twice, sometimes three times, a day. This extravagance made me feel ghetto rich. The life I saw advertised in music videos and magazines was a life I had managed to acquire through the street. Before then, I could only crave those high priced clothes, gold necklaces, and a fist full of money. I couldn't wait to return to Midway so I could show off my new possessions.

This motivated me to do what the School Away officials required from me. I turned in every assignment, passed every test, and didn't cause my teachers any problems. At the end of the school year I had passed all my classes and was recommended back to Midway.

When I returned next year, my name meant something more. I was not just Fabian Harper. I had entered that realm where myth and legend were blurred to become FABIAN HARPER. Young girls flocked to me, hoping I would be persuaded into being their boyfriend. But I refused any attention that the young black girls gave me. I couldn't break from those negative images I had of the two dominant black women in my life. My rejection of black girls led me to accepting Molly, who was white.

The first thing that caught my attention about Molly was her hair. She was a redhead, but instead of her hair being the large looping curls that I was used to seeing on redheads, it was long and straight. She did have freckles, and occasionally I teased her about them, saying they made her look like the comic book characters Archie and Annie. We spent our lunch breaks together talking and laughing. The black girls hated Molly and picked at her, and I too faced my share of ridicule, not from the boy students, however, but from my educators. My social studies teacher told me how disgraceful it was for me to be walking around school with that white girl, as she called Molly, when there were so many black "sisters" I could choose from. But I didn't see beautiful black girls; I only saw the women who had neglected me. The emptiness that I felt from their emotional absence directed my anger and hostility at black girls. Molly was safe.

I spent hours on the phone with Molly telling her the things young girls liked to hear, making false promises, and saying those words all girls her age seemed so easily to believe, "Of course I love you." But this was all a farce, a clever scheme to claim her highest prize. I wanted her sex and would tell her anything she wanted to hear until finally she broke with the remark, "I love you too."

I met her behind the school staircase during fifth period class. We were both excited, and after smiling at each other, we began kissing and grabbing, our fingers frantically working to unbuckle each other's pants, and pulling them down to our ankles, we lay on the floor and I went inside her.

We had forgotten about the time and where we were, when I heard a voice beside me say, "Fabian, get up."

Molly opened her eyes and said over my shoulder, "Mr. Lynn."

Hearing Molly call Mr. Lynn's name. I rolled off her, grabbing for my pants at my ankles.

"You two get dressed and follow me," he said.

We both were suspended pending a school board hearing. At the hearing, it was decided to let Molly back in school, but I was expelled and sent back to School Away.

I walked back into the admissions office of School Away and noticed nothing had changed. The building still held a smell of stale old clothes, the same dusty spider webs hung in the ceiling corners, and there was a draft in the building that gave me that same dire reminder of when I first felt it, that the big old house which now was a school was haunted. The same teachers were still there, as well as most of the old students. And my desk had remained empty, like it had been waiting for me to return to it.

Most people walking back into such familiarity would be pleasantly comfortable, but I wasn't. I hated School Away. It was a school of strict regimen. All boys were in the back half of the building while the girls' classes were toward the front. We all did our work in individual small cubicles. During class, the entire school was silent. No one talked, not even the teachers. As students, we were allowed to speak briefly with one another during our break for lunch. The school officials let no more than five of us break at one time, then we were ordered back into our little cubicles. Whenever a teacher entered our work station to check an assignment, we had to stand. We couldn't ask any questions unless given permission by the teacher. Such permission was only given to answer a teacher's question, and to answer that question only. No idle talk was allowed between us and the teachers. If we needed to use the restroom, a designated school worker would march us individually in silence right past students working in their cubicle to the restroom, and waited until we finished to walk us back to our work area. There were other rules that we followed. Though I didn't like being at School Away, if I had not been sent there, I would have failed the sixth and seventh grades. My loathing for the school kept me working hard to get back to Midway, which I returned to the following year.

Before the school year was fully under way, Mr. Lynn had a meeting with my mother and me in his office. He wanted to tell us that he was moving me on to the ninth grade.

"Since Fabian had outstanding grades at School Away," he told my mother, "it would be a waste of his skill to make him go through the eighth grade. Therefore, I recommend to the school board that they pass Fabian right to the ninth grade."

A smile stretched across my mother's face, but I just looked at the man. Despite what he said, I knew his real reason—he just wanted to get rid of me.

My mother drove me across town to register me in Captain Shreve High School, a school once attended by her, my aunts and uncles and cousins. Mr. Powell, the principal there, had coached my uncles in gym, and my athletic coach Mr. Reeves had blocked for one of my uncles on the school's football team. Pictures of my uncle's football playing days with the school and later with the Chicago Bears hung in the school's gym locker room as well as in the school's Hall of Fame cabinet. My aunt had been on the school's honor student list, and my cousin had been a track star. With such a heritage laid before me, Captain Shreve was supposed to be a fresh start. But I was poisoned with the lore of street survival, and ended up getting suspended for fighting. Mr. Powell sent me home and called my grandmother. When I got home, I was lectured by both her and my mother, who said they weren't going to stand for my embarrassing the family at that school. Family? I wasn't their family. My grandmother had made this clear to me long ago, and my mother had cast me aside for Edward, I felt. I had a family but it wasn't them, it was my gang.

If I could have grasped the chance I had at Captain Shreve, my life might have turned out differently. But the anger I had for my family caused me to reject everything that associated me with them. I had people whom I could identify with. This is why I continued around the gangs. Whenever my mother would mention that I needed to change my friends, I always had the rationale that she didn't have the right to tell me anything. I was raising myself. I can't say she never tried to talk to me, but it was too late. I was grown. I was hypnotized by my confidence in those people I sought to be a part of, believing their opinions were the ones that mattered.

Never did it enter my thought that those associates whom I had pledged my loyalty to would put me in the precarious predicament I found hard to escape from. A person was dead and another fighting for her life. And now my friends left me alone to get out of the mess.

I wasn't there when the shooting happened, yet Eric S——, my co-defendant , said I was there. No, I did not testify in my defense. I did not pay attention to the witnesses. I sat in court looking straight ahead because my lawyer told me looking at the jury would make them nervous. So I sat there trying not to move, praying, hoping, wanting to believe. But I was nervous, and my eyes followed the prosecutor as he moved across the courtroom, shaking the pistol at the jurors, yelling, stomping his feet, as he delivered his closing arguments. A black woman had been killed and another wounded during a robbery. Though she testified that there was only one person who shot her and her daughter, and since Eric had already pled guilty, I still sat there as the second person charged with the shootings.

I had told my lawyer no, I had nothing to do with it, that I was at home, opening the front door, when I saw the lady across the street get out of her car carrying grocery bags into her home at the exact time the crime was happening. She would normally have been at work, she wrote in her affidavit, but her father was sick, so that day she stayed home to care for him, and for me to see her, I had to have been at home also. I had turned on the television to the 12:00 news and saw a friend of Darren Sloan had been shot on Broadway, so I called Darren's house. His uncle answered and told me Darren was not there. I told my lawyer all of these things, but the jury heard none of it. My lawyer rested my case without putting me on the stand or calling a witness on my behalf. The jury only heard the prosecutor's side.

The prosecutor argued, "Ladies and gentlemen of the jury, the facts of this case are simple. I am sure that after you have heard me, you will find the defendant, Fabian Harper, guilty of second degree murder and attempted second degree murder. On September 5, 1990, Eric S——, his older brother Darren S——, and Fabian walked from Eric's grandmother's house to the pawn shop located at the corner of Greenwood Road and Jewella Avenue. Fabian said they should get a car and some money that day. All three of them made it to the pawn shop and went inside. While Darren was looking at some speakers, Fabian and Eric left and saw a low-rider truck turn off Jewella Avenue onto a street and saw it pull in front of a house. Fabian said he was going to get the keys and went to the carport door of the house. Fabian returned to say there were too many people at the house, so they left. At this time, Eric saw that Fabian had a 22-caliber pistol. As they walked back toward Jewella, they saw a small car with a handicapped license plate turn up to the house. Fabian went to the door, and Eric heard loud voices. Eric kept walking when, 'BANG!'" The prosecutor hollered, pointing the gun at the jurors. "'BANG!' Fabian shot two ladies. He then came running with a purse in his hand and told Eric he had just burned two people.

"Later that day, Eric was caught. The police found a check belonging to one of the ladies on him." The prosecutor closed his eyes, then raised his arms in the air, and said, "Thank God, ladies and gentlemen. If Eric hadn't had that check, we would not have caught this murderer," he said, pointing at me.

"At the police station, Eric told the police Fabian shot the ladies.

The police recovered the purse behind the Delta gas station about five blocks from the crime scene.

"Based upon the information provided by Eric, Fabian was arrested at his mother's home the next day. Eric told police that Fabian had hidden the gun in his yard and had thrown the shell casings in the neighbor's back yard. The police found the gun lying next to a tree.

"Ladies and gentlemen, I am confident you will look at these facts and find Fabian Harper guilty." The prosecutor sat down.

My lawyer stood up. "Ladies and gentlemen, it is obvious what has happened. The prosecutor has made a deal with the wrong boy. The prosecutor let Eric plea bargain to seven years to testify against my client. All the prosecutor wants is a conviction, even if it's the wrong boy.

"Now I am going to give you some facts. Fact: at the time of Eric's arrest, he had in his possession a check made payable to the victim. Fact: after the police arrested Eric, he took them to the scene of the crime, where he had discarded the victim's purse. Fact: a witness described seeing the perpetrator run from the house of the victim. Eric admitted he ran that way after the shooting. Fact: while at the parish jail, Eric wrote several letters admitting that he was the shooter. Fact: the surviving victim has testified that there was only one person at her door, the shooter. Fact: the most compelling fact of all is that the surviving victim herself took the stand and said, 'The prosecutor got the wrong man,' talking about my client Mr. Harper. She said, 'It's not him.' Then in front of you, in a video of a line-up that included my client and Eric, she picked out Eric as the shooter." He stopped to let his words sink into the jury's minds. "The only reason Fabian sits before you being tried is because he would not talk. The prosecutor gave Eric a deal for his testimony. He gave Eric seven years, which means he will only do three years in prison. Now I ask you to end this nightmare for my client. Let your decision be not guilty." My lawyer took his seat.

The judge gave the jury instructions, and it left to deliberate. My lawyer got up, went over to the prosecutor, and shook his hand.

"Nice job," he told the prosecutor.

"You didn't do bad yourself," the prosecutor responded.

"Say, you seen that juror's eyes when you pointed that gun at her?"

"Yeah. I thought for sure she would scream." They both laughed.

What? I thought of my lawyer. He's laughing and talking to the prosecutor like all of this is a game even though my life is on the line.

A few hours later, the jury returned. Their faces were stern. That made me nervous. The clerk took a piece of paper from the jury foreman's hand and handed it to the judge.

"Stand, Mr. Harper," he said.

The courtroom was quiet. The judge put on his glasses and read, "For the count of attempted murder, we, the jury, find the defendant, Fabian Harper, not guilty. For the count of murder, we the jury find the defendant, Fabian Harper, guilty."

How could they find me not guilty, then guilty? I didn't understand. I stood there stunned. That was 1990. I have been in prison ever since, with no money, no help, no nothing. And those Gideons just left my cell telling me there's a God. I can still see the look on my jury's faces when the verdict was read. I could swear one of them smiled at me.

I heard a light sound of metal tapping against my cell bars. I opened my eyes and saw a guard standing outside my cell holding a pair of leg shackles and handcuffs.

"You got doctor clinic," he said.

Slowly, I got up from my bunk, and walked up to the cell bars where I stuck my hands out through the bars. The guard clamped the handcuffs down on my wrist so I could not pull my hands back into the cell, and after I turned around, he locked my hands behind my back with the handcuffs.

"Rack it back!" he hollered out to the tier at the guard behind the controls.

My cell door squeaked slowly back and the guard moved aside to let me walk out of the cell. I carefully moved my feet so the steel shackles wouldn't cut into the skin of my ankles. I took small shuffling steps as I went up the tier. The guard slowly walked six steps behind me. All the guards did this. Just in case a prisoner in a cell decided to douse you with shit as you passed him, the guards didn't want to get hit. Or if needle darts were being spat at you from a cell, the guards walked far enough behind to insure a dart didn't stick him.

I made it to the lobby and a guard there opened the lobby's steel door so I could go through it. The guard then followed close behind me. As I walked up the walkway toward the doctor's clinic, I thought about how none of us at Camp J ever left our cells without being handcuffed, shackled, and guarded. We couldn't even walk to the shower without being chained down and guarded, though the shower was only at the front of the tier and each of us showered alone. Not being able to leave my cell without handcuffs and shackles and with a guard behind my back depressed me so that I hardly left my cell the entire time I was at Camp J. Instead, I took baths out of my toilet, did push-ups on my cell floor for exercise, and whenever I felt sick, I would treat myself with aspirin or Maalox I ordered through sick call.

Inside the doctor's clinic, I sat at a chair by the nurse's desk and waited for her to finish the conversation she was having with a guard. They talked about the execution that would take place later that night.

"I thought he got a stay," she said.

"I hope not," he said. "The way he butchered that man, they should've put him down."

I looked at him. He was fat and short, with a receding hairline. He reminded me of the Penguin on Batman. The thought ran through my mind that he couldn't have had a woman at home and he was standing there trying to impress upon the nurse that he was a "bad" guard. I thought he was a pathetic and sad representation of a man. He must be desperate, I remember thinking, because the nurse wasn't worth it. She looked like a rag doll; she had her stringy black hair in a ball at the top of her head, and it looked like tumbleweed with strings of it sticking out. Her white tennies had dried mud around their edges, she had brown stained teeth, from nicotine no doubt, and she was as skinny as a broom. He had to be desperate.

"Oh well," she said, then looked at me. "What you here for?"

"I don't know," I said. "Ya'll called me over here."

"D.O.C."

"33 63 74."

She hit some keys on the computer she sat in front of and then said to me, "Oh, you made several sick calls asking for Maalox."

"Yeah."

"Your chest hurts."

60

"No."

Her fingers struck a few more keys, then a small white card came from the printer next to the computer. She handed me the card and pointed, "Go through that door."

I got up and walked through the door into a small doctor's room. He was a foreigner who barely spoke English.

"Hop on table," he told me, and as I did so, he took the card from my hand and read it.

"You having chest pains?" he asked.

"No."

"You requested lots of Maalox."

"They can't cook."

"I listen to your blood pressure, OK."

He grabbed my wrist and looked at his watch. After several seconds he gave me his diagnosis.

"You have high blood pressure," he said. "I put you on meds two times a day."

I nodded my head. Was he crazy? There was no way I was trusting his findings after one minute of only checking my pulse. I hadn't been in Angola that long; however, I had already heard the rumors of how Angola doctors used us as guinea pigs for experimental drugs. If the drug worked that was fine, but if it killed us they needed the bed space anyhow. These thoughts were firmly fixed in my mind so there was no way I was taking any kind of meds he prescribed, not even vitamins. However, I could not tell the doctor that, or it would be seen as if I was refusing medical treatment. And if you refused medical help, it would be a long time before any doctor saw you again. So the method was to accept the medicine when the lady guard brought it to my cell and when she left, toss the pills in the toilet.

I hopped down from the table and walked out of the room.

When I got back to my cell I found my sheets had been ripped off my bed and thrown on the floor; shoe prints were on them. My toilet paper was open and my mattress was rolled back on the bunk. A guard had been in my cell, shaking it down. They did that every time we left our cells for any reason. Because most prisoners did not like anyone touching their things, many prisoners saw the guards' intrusion as a violation of their space and hated it. The guards knew this, so any time we left our cells they went in them. Most of the guards hated being bothered; they just wanted to sit on their butts and wait for their shift to be off. So going in our cells was a way they used to discourage us from asking for our rec time or shower. I kept nothing in my cell; therefore, I didn't care if the guards searched it down every day, and as the guard was taking the handcuffs off me, I asked him to let me use the telephone.

"You used it this month?" he asked.

"No."

He hesitated a moment as he unfastened the last handcuff, then said, "We'll see."

That meant no. The guards rarely wanted to take time off of their doing nothing to let us use the telephone. The reason was that they had to handcuff and shackle us, walk us down the tier to the phone, and stand there while we talked. So when he said "We'll see," I knew not to ask him again. We were only allowed one fifteen-minute call a month. To ask him again risked aggravating him. Most of the guards when they got upset with you for repeatedly asking to use the phone would write it down in their log book that they let you use it, and in doing that you lost your month's phone call. Knowing this, I waited to catch another guard.

At 2:00 that morning a guard let me out to use the phone. I was chained down with shackles and handcuffs. Because the phone was at the end of tier, rules prohibited the guard from removing a handcuff to let me dial a number. And since the phone was on the floor behind the lobby bars, I had to lie on the floor and stretch my hand out between the bars and hope my finger tip hit the right numbers. Because as soon as I stopped dialing the guard wrote down that I had made contact. Luckily I did.

My mother answered the phone on the first ring. That surprised me; I thought for sure she was resting for work. She told me that Billy, my stepfather, had died and she had already called Angola to make arrangements for me to attend the funeral. Then she asked me how I felt.

"Fine," I told her. "I actually had been preparing myself for his death."

That was true. The day I found out that he was drinking again I told myself he would die soon. So the news of his death didn't bother me.

Getting to the funeral home took six and a half hours. During the entire ride to Shreveport I was handcuffed, shackled, and had a chain wrapped around my waist. You would think that the trip had been uncomfortable, but I hardly noticed. My eyes were open for the entire trip, taking in buildings, passing new model cars, and the scenery.

We arrived at the funeral home at 12:00 noon. Guests and family were arriving. When the guards let me out of the van, some of them stared at me. I put my head down as I walked chained with two armed guards trailing me into the funeral home, and I took my seat in the back of the chapel. As people began filing in, they walked past me, staring. Some stopped to give me a hug or to ask how I was doing, but most of them just cut their eyes at me as they walked by. My mother and sister came and hugged me. "Only one hug apiece," the guard told them. His words have stuck with me all these years, for they tell of the sad and lonely feeling of that day. None of my other family members came over to me. They walked past me as if I didn't exist, like they had never known me. And as the service proceeded, I sat in the back of that chapel watching my mother and sister crying. I desperately wanted to be with them to comfort them, but I couldn't. I was a prisoner. I had to sit alone with the guards. During the ride back to Angola I thought about that— sitting alone in that pew. I began thinking about my case.

"I didn't even see my lawyer's face until the day of the trial," I had said to myself. "And my jury? How could they believe Eric? I know they heard the lady say it wasn't me who shot her and her daughter, but that it was Eric." I flopped my head back on the seat, took in a deep breath, then let it go. "Nine and a half hours. That's how long it took them to find me not guilty of attempted murder. But then they find me guilty of attempted murder! I don't understand. I shook my head. "If only juror number four hadn't changed his vote then I would have gotten a mistrial. Juror number four. That's it. JUROR NUMBER FOUR! Something happened in that jury room, but what?" The van brakes squeaked to a halt.

"You're home," the guard said, then got out of the van and walked around it to let me out.

As I stepped out of the van I could hear the familiar sounds of men's voices arguing on the tiers. "I got to get outta this place." I mumbled to myself as I started up the walkway. "God, if you're real…."

I made it back to my cell as last chow was being served. A prisoner who worked the tiers brought me a tray. I looked at the small servings of food in the tray slots and shook my head. Camp J kitchen fed us just enough to keep us breathing. If you went there weighing 200 pounds, you were guaranteed to leave having lost 60 of those pounds. I have met people back there who said they intentionally put themselves in J just so they could lose weight. I wasn't one of those people, and I wanted some food on my tray. Apparently another prisoner up the tier was as equally disgusted with the small amount of food as I was because he kept hollering for the guards.

"What!" a guard snapped, standing in front of the prisoner's cell.

"I want some food on my tray," the prisoner yelled back.

"You called me for that?" the guard snapped. "Eat what you got and don't call me no more."

"Fuck you! You eat it." Then I heard the plastic tray hit against the tier wall. The prisoner had thrown his tray. I waited and listened. No sound. Then boots came running into the tier. I looked out onto the tier through my tray hatch and saw what I expected to see. Ten to twelve huge white men in solid black fatigues. They were the tact (cell entrance) team. They wore helmets, carried black iron shields, and twirled black sticks. Nobody on the tier said anything. We simply listened, and the guard whom the prisoner had thrown the tray at told the prisoner to come to the bars and be handcuffed.

"Come in and get me."

"You're not coming up here?"

"No."

Most might question not going to the bars to be handcuffed, but any smart prisoner knew better than to do that. Your ass was going to get beaten whether you cooperated or not. So it was better to get whipped with your hands free than with them locked behind your back; that way at least you could get a few punches in on them yourself. Go down swinging, as we used to say.

The guard stepped aside for the tact crew. One of the black suited guards held a large canister and black hose in his hand. The canister was filled with pepper spray.

"Stand back!" he said, and the other guards formed a double line behind him. He pointed the hose of the canister at the cell and pulled its trigger. It sounded like that guard was spraying a fire extinguisher. A large white cloud floated down the tier, engulfing all of us inside our cells. I hurried and wet my towel to cover my mouth and nose. You didn't want to inhale that spray, it choked you. And I heard prisoners in their own cells gagging, coughing, and sneezing.

"Rack it back!" the guard yelled and as the door slowly rolled back, those guards rushed the prisoner inside his cell. From my cell I could hear grunts, bodies banging against the cell wall, and the soles of the guards' boots squeaking on the concrete floor, and I heard that prisoner's yell.

"C'mon motherfuckers! Augh! You got me! Damn—" He had had enough.

The guards dragged him out of the cell onto the tier while he was kicking out at them. All of the guards then tackled him and held him as another guard handcuffed and shackled him. Then grabbing hold of the chain of the shackles, one of the guards drug him off the tier into the lobby where they beat him some more. I heard that prisoner hollering and shouting all the way down to my cell.

"Damn you all!" he yelled. "Damn you all to hell!"

For the rest of my time back there I never saw that prisoner again.

Later that same night when it came time for the guards to shower us, one of them came down the tier putting a cigarette in each of our cells' tray hatch. He was buying our shower time. This was something that was done often. The guards hated working. They just wanted to come in, sit on their butts and talk, pull their twelve hours, and leave. They hated doing anything. And since showering us required them to do some work, them knowing that most of the tier smoked but we weren't allowed to have any cigarettes, it was a perfect trade. I didn't care, because like many prisoners do throughout the prison, I bathed out of my toilet or sink anyhow. I was just ready to leave.

Over the next months I sat in my cell thinking, reading, writing, as I waited on the day to be released back into population. That day soon came when two guards, one a captain and the other a classification officer, stood in front of my cell. This was the board I had been waiting on. The prisoner in the cell next to me had told me about the two guards that held the board. "Just agree with everything they say," he told me, and I did. "And when they ask you a question, lie."

"They don't want to hear the truth," he told me. "They want to hear something related to penitentiary bullshit."

I had confided in him how I ended up at J, and he quickly let me know that the board would never go for my story. "They will never believe someone planted a knife on you," he said. Instead, he told me to play on the fact that I had just come to prison and tell them that a prisoner was messing with me about my ass. I was reluctant to take his advice, but I wanted to get back from there. So I did as he suggested, and guess what, it worked.

Chapter 3

After I had done a year at Camp J, I was sent back to C block. Some of the same prisoners were still there. My mother used to say to me that a lie will walk a mile before the truth decides to lift its sleeping head off the pillow. I never gave thought to her cliché until I pushed my metal locker boxes into the cell with a new cellmate, Craig.

Word had already spread that I used to be Raymond's cellmate, and naturally prisoners looked at me as I walked down the tier. The excitement in their eyes told me that they hoped I was another Raymond. In prison once a rumor is attached to you, no matter if it's not true, it sticks to you your entire incarceration. The rumor that had circulated about me before I went to camp J was that I had potential to be a prison fuck boy. When Raymond started exchanging sex for food and clothes, many prisoners reasoned that since they were screwing Raymond and we were cellmates, I was already having sex with him in the cell but had kept quiet about it because I didn't want him to expose that he was fucking me. In their lustful drive to try to conquer me, they overlooked that I had stopped talking to Raymond shortly after his new occupation, and I was about to move out of the cell. These things, however, were dismissed with simple logic. My "pretend" attempt to get moved was only a smoke screen to conceal that Raymond was fucking me. They even got Raymond to say things that helped to add spice to this lie.

Such perverted thinking is born out of penitentiary philosophies promoted by older prisoners. Many of them cannot think beyond the prison walls. Their reasoning is confined to concepts of a phantom prison code. Young prisoners, when they start interacting in the prison general population, will adopt the warped principles set by those older prisoners, thus ensuring that the cycle of debilitating ideas are carried on into the next generation of young prisoners. I became a victim of those ideas.

When the cell door closed I stood looking into the eyes of a man in his early forties. His weight topped mine by about two hundred pounds. Looking at him, I could tell that he used to lift weights, but his muscles had become soft from lack of work. That no doubt was because he had spent a lot of time in the cell, waiting. That the cell was clean and neat and his shoes lined against the wall told me that he had been doing time for a while—23 years, he told me later.

As I began unpacking my boxes, he tried to start a conversation with me. At first I resisted any effort at communication, but gradually, over days, I found myself responding to the things he would say: "You think the Lakers gonna make the playoffs?" "Man, Clinton, you know he smoked that weed." "You know how the Supreme Court ruled in Cage vs. Louisiana?" These topics always sparked a debate between us, and we would spend nights arguing over which basketball player was the greatest, how to interpret court rulings, and whether the governor would sign our pardons. Our conversations soon drifted to our lives. He casually would ask me questions about what my life was like before prison. I told him how I used to always fight at school, that I had to get a job at twelve, that I didn't have many friends except V.C. I made sure, however, not to say that V.C. was gay or hint at how close we were. While I talked, Craig would sit on his bed or on the edge of the toilet and listen to me attentively, as if he was a counselor and I was his patient. He even shared moments about his life stories I am convinced now were made up to gain my trust. I have since learned that what Craig did with me was a common ruse many older prisoners use on young prisoners. Their invented stories, politeness, and supposed acts of genuine concern are ploys to win a young prisoner's confidence. Through these skits, it is the older prisoner's goal to get the young prisoner to lower his resistance. The older one will use his established line of communication to prod at the younger prisoner until he discovers what his interests are; then he will become the main caterer to those interests. The older prisoner will come to the defense of the young prisoner against others, lend his last dollar without demanding payment back, and with the help of other prisoners, stage conflicts so he can help the young prisoner resolve them. All of these schemes are used so he can draw the young prisoner close to him, to get the younger person to see him as a friend. Once that is accomplished, the older prisoner begins to lead the younger into discussions about sexual gratification. This entire process may be simple, but, nevertheless, clever methods are devised by older prisoners. And I am sure Craig had practiced on other cellmates before he met me.

Once Craig got me talking about my sexual cravings, he would interject his thoughts for satisfying those desires. Sometimes I would respond with a crazy answer that we both would laugh at. Other times I would remain quiet, especially when I thought his commands were targeted at me. Then one afternoon, after coming in from a work half, Craig confronted me about the rumor.

"I know you and Raymond were fucking each other," he told me, "so stop playing games with me."

I looked straight at him. A part of me was mad at him for believing a rumor, since he had been incarcerated long enough to know that prisoners will lie to each other about anything, especially if it furthers their own devious motives. But I was more angry at myself for thinking that he was genuine, when I knew that most older prisoners' minds were corroded with so-called convict logic. Looking back, I guess that I knew Craig would test my explanations, but I had wanted to believe he was different. Maybe that is why I had hoped to explain my way out of his advances, but nothing I said was anything he wanted to hear. All he wanted to know was why I wouldn't "bless" him, a term prisoners use to ask another prisoner to suck his penis. But when I told him, "I don't suck dicks," his response was, "I'm not asking you to suck no one else's, only mine."

I shook my head. I knew what I had to do.

"Look," he said, "I'm not going to tell nobody. What we do in our cell is nobody's business but ours." Then he unbuckled his belt and started to pull his pants down. When he bent over to push them past his knees, I swung my skinny arms, hitting him as hard as I could. He grabbed hold of me and we wrestled for about two minutes, until a guard walked down the corridor to make a visual count and saw us fighting. Because I had thrown the first punch, I was sent back to lockdown for another eight months.

Since that fight with Craig, I have come in contact with other prisoners who tried to pass themselves off as kind and caring but were really predators using whatever tactic they could to get acquainted with me. But that fight with Craig taught me never to trust another prisoner again.

I see new prisoners come in, and there are those who still play the game of older vs. younger prisoner. True, gone are the days when a young prisoner came to Angola and was brutally raped. Though I imagine there are unreported rapes still occurring in these cells, what a young prisoner experiences today is better likened to charming than rape. Whether a prisoner has been in Angola for a long period or a few years, to win that "special friend," many will use the art of verbal persuasion or wooing with material treats to proposition young prisoners. "It'll be only between us," they will say. "You got my word, I ain't telling nobody." Some prisoners will engage in sex if they feel comfortable that no one will find out. Sometimes their secret will remain hidden, but usually it won't. However, for those young prisoners who say "No" or appear ready to fight, that pretty much will end an older prisoner's advances. But there is something that the young prisoner misses. He wrongly assumes that such pursuits are only about sex. What most of these older prisoners are after is something to soothe the poignant pain of incarceration. They gain satisfaction being able to spend some time with a young prisoner walking the rec yard, smoking weed, laughing and talking, showering with him, innocently touching his hands or patting him on the shoulder, eating with him in the kitchen or playing basketball—all provide the older prisoner with enough mental sexual stimulus to satisfy his physical urges. That is not to say that if the young prisoner decides to bend over, the other will not fuck him. But in these "secret" love affairs, victory is not in the kill but in the catch

Chapter 4

"Single file to the right," he yelled out as we walked, passing him by the door. Then he blew his whistle. "SINGLE FILE TO THE RIGHT!"

We began filing to the right in a single line on our way to the kitchen. I could smell the gravy and scratch biscuit being cooked, and their aroma led me to a line of hungry prisoners waiting to be fed. We were served two biscuits and a shot of gravy, with an eight ounce glass of milk. Guards stood around in the kitchen, and as we ate, they walked around our tables hollering at us to hurry. They needed us fed and out of the kitchen by 6:30, time enough for us to make it out to the bullpen for 7:00 check out. So they harassed us to finish eating.

"Drink that milk up!" a guard yelled in the direction of the table where I sat. The prisoner seated across from me stood up, guzzling down his milk, then hurried for the door.

I walked over to the bullpen with the other prisoners. I never got used to the bullpen's smell—a stinking mix of funky bodies, mud, and horse piss. Turning up my lip, I looked around and saw a couple new prisoners. They had been sent straight down the walk from the reception center. Like me when I first tasted the dust of the fields, they were young, innocent to the exhaustive labor of field work. On their feet were hard brogans, their jeans were still starched stiff, and they wore the blue long-sleeved shirts the prison hands out to us every six months. I looked at them and thought, "They are gonna burn up in the heat." Since I was now a veteran of field work, I wore a white t-shirt, an old pair of jeans, and tennis shoes. I also wore a straw sombrero—it was right for blocking the sun, but I still sweated heavily under it.

I was standing quietly, waiting for the bullpen guard to start calling roll, when one of the new prisoners nudged me.

"What type of work they gonna have us doing?" he asked.

"Don't know," I responded. "Every day it's something different."

"Do we…"

"Shhh. You have to listen for your number."

The bullpen guard had started calling our numbers. One by one we walked through the check out gate answering, and began forming a line on the dirt road that ran in front of the bullpen. We were a vegetable picking line, so none of us needed tools.

Once we were lined up, our linepusher, who was at the head of the line on horseback, hollered out, "Walk it!" and we started our long walk out to the fields. We walked at a fast pace, working up a sweat that ran in steady streams down my face until finally we stopped at an acre field of nothing but rows of shrubs with tiny green peppers.

"All right," our linepusher said, "I don't want to ride down your row and see a pepper left on a bush. If I do, I will have something for you. Now get to work."

I settled on a row and began to pick. The sun stung the back of my neck, and my fingers cramped as I worked them vigorously, snapping peppers off the branches. We worked for a straight two hours, filling up five gallon buckets with peppers, when our linepusher finally decided to give us a break. A few prisoners headed to the cooler that was in the middle of the field for water; others walked over to a drainage ditch, unzipped their pants, tilted their heads back, and let loose. I had walked a few paces from my row, twisting and bending, trying to work out the dull pain I felt in my lower back from bending over, when I heard a prisoner by the ditch shout, "This is torture!" Such bursts of frustration are common. "There ought to be a law against working us like this," he continued.

Suddenly, the linepusher called me back to my row. "What's that, Harper?" he asked, pointing at a pepper on a bottom branch.

"Oh," I said, then reached down and plucked off the pepper.

He looked at me. "You got a ticket," he said, and walked away. The ticket was a write-up. When he handed it to me, it read that I had failed to pick my row of peppers with "reasonable speed and efficiency." "What is reasonable speed and efficiency?" I wondered. I held that write-up in my hand, the anger boiling inside of me… it was a good thing that the morning work half was over, or I would have told him to "Call the truck," a phrase I had often found myself saying to linepushers whenever I chose to go to the hole instead of continuing working.

When I got back to my dormitory, I lay on the floor next to my bed. Some prisoners went to change out of their sweaty clothes, a ritual like they do before walking to the kitchen. But I was too beat to move, at least not until the whistle blew for chow. I slowly got to my feet and headed out the door to the kitchen with the other prisoners.

You would have thought eating in a hot kitchen was aggravating enough, but looking at prisoners serving our food with sweat dripping from their chins into the pots, and having to fan away gnats and flies as we were yelled at by guards to hurry and eat is enough to try the patience of any man.

I ate my food, then got out of there and went back to my dorm to await the whistle for the second half of work duty.

Besides the once-a-year Arts and Crafts Festival, other events have come along which allow us to feel important to the outside world. One of those times was when a movie crew came to film the motion picture *Out of Sight*, and they needed inmate extras. At first no one wanted to participate, but a rumor started to circulate that one of the film stars, Jennifer Lopez, was going to be at the location where the movie was being filmed. Each time the rumor passed through another inmate, something new was added. Soon everyone believed that Jennifer Lopez wanted to meet her extra help. The possibility of being released could not have excited us more than the opportunity to gaze lustfully upon Jennifer Lopez. When the release form came around for us to sign, so many wrote their names down that security had to select who would be extras. I was one of the lucky ones to be chosen.

That morning was cold. All 500 of us wore blue jean coats as we were escorted in a line to Cellblock B yard, and there on the basketball court, where inmates usually play games of four on four, was George Clooney. Contrary to the rumor, there was no Jennifer Lopez. But that was OK, that rare opportunity to be in a movie excited us still. Before George Clooney, I had never come eye to eye with a movie star. He was then a man of middle age, rather short, who wore his gray-white hair combed to a part on the side. He wore the same prison blue shirt that we were wearing, stiff blue jeans, and a pair of brown leather brogans. He looked like a regular prisoner, but he didn't act like one of us. He moved among us smiling, shaking hands, and casually chatting with us as if he were a host at a dinner party and we were his guests. We enjoyed him.

Another actor in the movie who grabbed the attention of most inmates was Lucy. He was playing the role of a prison homosexual. He was coconut white, thin, dressed in a blue shirt unbuttoned to his chest with the ends of the shirt tied together in a bow, and he wore his blue jeans two sizes too small to reveal the curves of his small butt. His hair was charcoal black and wavy, his eyebrows were arched high over his black eyes, and I don't know if he was aware of it, but when he walked he slung his hips in such a way that his small round butt cheeks bounced up, then down, with each step. This hypnotized some of the inmates. He tried to explain that he was simply a good actor and not homosexual, but they didn't hear him. The way some of the inmates gawked, if no guards had been there, I imagined that the small crowd would have broken out in a frenzy and some would have attacked and ravished him, even while some of us stood around watching.

The movie director told us that we had to take off our coats. We didn't want to mainly because none of us wanted to risk facing retribution from the prison administration for this. But we did and the director told us what he wanted us to do:

"While George is playing basketball, I want some of you to stand around the court hollering as if you're cheering for the game. The rest of you I want standing around watching these men play checkers." I stood next to the checker players.

When the camera started rolling, I couldn't shake the feeling that I was part of something great and was mildly excited by this, and when the movie finally came out on video, I sat in front of the TV with the same excitement of that day. When I saw my face in the first scene of the movie, I couldn't help feeling important.

Chapter 5

To physically survive in prison, you must live with a constant sense that there is danger. Security can't guard everywhere, and though for the most part we get along, there are people and situations that you are wise to avoid. Though someone isn't being killed every day, there are fights between prisoners, some severe. Fights between security officers also happen. As for sex, that is a prevailing topic among prisoners. Some will find themselves a mate in another prisoner. It's almost impossible for them to find a place to be alone, and once I remember a prisoner hung his sheets down around his bed and crawled on the floor beneath them with his companion. Soon you heard a belt buckle clink against the cement floor, there was a brief moment of silence, then sounds of low hand claps and grunts came from under the bed, and I saw silhouetted on the sheets one of the prisoner's hips thrusting up and down on the other prisoner's butt.

If they stayed under there too long, this usually brought whispers from other prisoners that the two prisoners were taking turns fucking each other. Such gossip is common. It's what most prisoners do, sit around and watch, then convene in small groups to shoo shoo about what they saw or heard for the day. Primarily discussed in these sessions is who are whores. And if a particular prisoner wasn't already a whore, then he was marked by other prisoners as a potential whore. Very few escaped some speculation, not even the prison jocks and religionists, though it was an unspoken rule among gossipers to guard what they said around those groups. Still, to those prisoners who sat gossiping, everyone was a "gal boy" except for themselves, and they loved spreading such rumors.

The rumors that came from these gossipers were called Hot Cow, and were funneled through what prisoners called the Angola Grapevine. The grapevine passed hot love-rumors between prisoners living in different parts of the prison. Each of the rumors that came through the grapevine was inaccurate, but that didn't matter. Right or wrong, prisoners love to hear the latest tales. I used to think that such nonsense only went on in the cellblocks where the only activity was watching one another, but down the walk in the dorms, such gossipmongers were worse.

When I hit the walk I usually tried to get along with the other prisoners. Since I am black, I naturally gravitated toward the black prisoners, and because we were forced to get along, I often took the toleration approach. Sometimes I would walk the yard or eat with another black prisoner in the chow hall, and in none of the conversations had I ever been propositioned for sex. But then I would catch in the wind that the one whom I had talked to or had eaten with was going around telling people I was going to let him fuck me. I could imagine the conversation.

"I saw you talking to Fabian."

"Yeah, I was hollering at the bitch."

"You trying to get some of that?"

"Oh. He'll let me hit."

"No shit!"

"Yeah, but he just don't want me to tell nobody."

"Still trying to hide behind that Bible, huh?"

"Yeah, the bitch using up the Bible."

I hated this. But there was no defense against those rumors. Such talk made me so disgusted with black prisoners that I gradually stopped communicating with all of them except for Leslie Young, Joe Whitehead, and Weldon Williams; their association was sincere. But I guarded myself against all other black prisoners because I saw in their eyes their ulterior motives. The old security guards used to joke that the reason blacks wouldn't run off was because we couldn't take our punks or penitentiary men with us.

When I first heard that joke it angered me; it showed how little sense security thought blacks possessed. However, the longer I did time, the more I saw how security could regard blacks so low. Most of the black prisoners seemed to think little about their freedom and bettering themselves academically, but instead seemed to be consumed with only three things: whores, sports, and making someone into a whore. Their thinking disgusted me so that I began hanging around the white boys.

The general rule around prison was blacks and whites did not associate unless drugs, gambling, or sex were involved. Since all the blacks knew that I didn't gamble or use drugs, it was concluded that I was providing sex to the whites. It never occurred to those blacks that I shared a bond with whites beyond the prisoners' code of perverted logic. Simple interests like watching the news, reading the A section of a newspaper, or talking about sensible things instead of penitentiary bullshit was my reason, and aside from this, I did like some of them. But the blacks didn't believe this. They had tagged me a "sweet boy"; thus they couldn't believe that my mind expanded beyond the imaginary barriers they lived behind, and it angered them to see me walking the yard laughing with whites or playing a game of volleyball with them. Blacks interpreted my close association with whites as a sign that I was openly courting the white population. To be honest, the only blacks that were upset with me for my acquaintance with whites were those who participated in homosexuality. No other blacks cared or gave much thought to my associations. As for those black homosexuals, they were angered simply because they were missing out on a piece of the action with me. If I would just sex blacks, too, one of them wrote to me in a letter left on my locker box, all would be fine. But if I didn't and continued to fuck whites, there would be trouble. The loathing I felt for that prisoner....

Refusing to be dictated to by prisoner policy, I continued to hang out with the whites. Those black homosexuals' stupidity fueled me to flaunt in their faces whatever type of relationship they thought I had going on with the whites. I would purposely walk past them with a white, laughing and talking, and I caught their glares as we passed by. But I didn't care. I began to see black homosexuals for what they really were, a bunch of institutionalized niggers who deserved to be locked away for the duration of their lives. The way I saw those men affected me so that the compassion I once felt for black prisoners slowly eroded, and I now hated all of them and wanted nothing to do with any prisoner who was black. Meanwhile, my so-called flirting with the whites brought the black homosexuals' frustration with me to a boil, and I eventually had to fight one of them. I will never forget walking up to him on the walk and hitting him in front of his friends, knocking him out.

After that fight I recall a black prisoner telling me that whites were weak and just as ignorant as the blacks whom I despised. It is true that a majority of the whites' minds seemed to be on how to stay loaded, and where most blacks saw all whites as whores, most whites regarded blacks as intellectually stupid and rats. I learned, however, when I crossed color lines, that there were just as many dumb whites as blacks, and a lot of whites were rats as well. And though most blacks saw whites as whores, the truth was there were just as many black sneak freaks (those who went both ways in sex behind closed doors, but in public act as if they would never participate) as there were whites. The only marked difference I observed between most black and white prisoners was that blacks had a tendency to display rudeness and flair, a bravado image, whereas whites tended to be quiet, reserved, sneaky. But for all the whites' shortcomings, they never caused me the grief blacks had. It was black faces I would see peeping in the shower from the walkway, trying to look at my naked body. Blacks were the ones who pried open the lids of my locker boxes, stealing my trial transcript and tearing it to shreds, then flushing the pieces down the toilet. And it was a black I fought for trying to masturbate me in the shower, for if I didn't fight, I would be looked at as weak by other blacks, and they would try the same. Only with blacks have I had to stand on the yard trading insult for insult, and it was only blacks who went behind my back lying to their friends that I was "their people," a phrase used among prisoners to classify me as being romantically involved with them. I would have expected prisoners whose nicknames were Whitey, Cracker, Redneck, Lightning Bolt, Trailer Trash, Cajun, Hillbilly, Ghost, and Hitler to attempt the things done to me by blacks, but they never did. Such behavior only came from my so-called "brothers." But for all the legal stress blacks caused me, they never managed to extinguish my spirit. I always managed to stay motivated working on my legal papers, trying to feel a way out of prison. However, fighting back my inner demons of doubt and frustration became more difficult each time I received bad news from court. The whisper "Give up," hollered within me the day I received bad news from home.

One time I was hit with bad news from court and home together. I had been anxiously awaiting a ruling from Court when finally it came in the mail. I can still recall the nervous flutter I felt in the pit of my stomach when the dorm guard called my name for mail. Months had passed since I stayed awake all night pecking out my writing on a manual typewriter and saved enough of my incentive wages to purchase stamps, then dropped the sealed envelope into the mailbox addressed to the First District Judicial Court.

When I took the envelope from the guard, I went back to my bed, and frantically worked my fingers beneath the crack of the envelope lip, leaving it open. I anxiously flipped to the last page, "DENIED." My heart sank. How? Turning back to the first page, I began to read the testimony of my co-defendant of how I shot the two ladies. "What!" I said to myself. "How can they believe him?" What about one of the ladies testifying that it wasn't me, but who had identified him as the shooter? How about the detective who testified that he believed it was my co-defendant and his brother who had testified to him that he shot the ladies? What about the letters Eric wrote to his brother on how he was going to pin the crimes on me? Angry, confused, I tore the papers in half. "Damn judges!"

I lit a cigarette, then lay back on my bed, staring at two men standing across from me talking. Right then, my eyes became blurry. I inhaled hard, opening my mouth to breathe out. I looked at the torn pieces of paper, scattered on my bed, and tears started sliding down my face. "I ain't never gonna get out," I thought.

The cigarette was unfiltered and too strong, it made me cough. The men laughed hysterically, their lips jerked back and forth exposing their coffee stained teeth. I wasn't focused on what they were laughing about. My mind instead replayed the scene of the last day of my trial. The clerk held the verdict paper down beside her leg to let me read the words "Not guilty," but then the judge's voice echoed in my head for count two: GUILTY. My throat, which was sore from coughing, hardly hurt, but my eyes burned from holding back tears. I didn't want the men standing across from me to look and see me crying, and I became angry at myself for crying at all.

I lay there and thought about my other court denials, and how the denial I had just received affected me. I took another pull from the cigarette, then stood up and walked outside where I opened my eyes wide to let the cool breeze blow them dry. I told myself that I wasn't going to let the denial get to me. I would be upset, but I wasn't going to cry anymore. I had faced disappointments all my life; it was stupid to cry. I plucked away the cigarette, then started my walk around the rec yard.

Three weeks after I got that denial, I received news that my grandmother had died. I will never forget talking on the phone to my mother that day She was crying, and I was trying to say the right words to comfort her, but I was falling to pieces inside. When I hung up the phone I broke down.

That night as I sat on my bed by the window in the darkened dormitory, the thought of my grandmother's death overwhelmed me again. And as I had done earlier that day when I heard the news, I analyzed my thoughts that week of her death, wondering if I had missed a sign that was warning me. Maybe if I had listened to my inner voice telling me to call her earlier that week. Maybe I could have reminded her to take her heart medication. Perhaps when she had told me on the phone that at Thanksgiving she would never see me out alive was a message good-bye, that in my stubbornness, I ignored. Could she have been saved? Had the paramedics done everything they could to revive her? There were no solid answers. The whole event was too painful to think about clearly. I recall feeling alone, sick, disappointed with myself for being in prison.

My mother told me that she could call Angola administrators to see if I could attend the funeral. I remember not wanting to go to the funeral dressed like a prisoner, looking on like an outcast. I wanted to dress human. The only person I knew who owned a nice pair of jeans was my friend Toby, but he was on the West Yard. They were not allowed to carry clothes through the gates, so I sent him a message to meet me at the education building that night wearing a pair of jeans he goes to visit in. There we would exchange jeans.

The education building was like a transit building for us prisoners. It was erected as a place we could go to to participate in self-help programs, but at night it was where prisoners from both yards met up to exchange drugs, information, cigarettes, sex, and whatever else they thought important. I was there to get Toby's jeans.

When Toby got there, we immediately went up the stairs, passing a black prisoner on our way to the second floor of the building. That prisoner had cut his eyes at us as we passed by him, but I really didn't give his look a thought. My mind was on swapping jeans with Toby.

Finding an empty classroom, I turned on the light and we went inside.

"We got to hurry up," I said.

"Man, sorry to hear about your grandmother."

"Thanks."

As Toby began to unbuckle his jeans, a guard came in.

"What ya'll doing?"

"Ah, nothing," I said. "We…" and then I saw his face fill with anger.

"Goddamn whores!"

"Huh?"

Each guard carried a walkie-talkie. On it was a button for them to press that sent out a signal for other guards' walkie-talkies in the area alerting them to come to a guards' aid when two prisoners are fighting. The guard pressed his beeper on us.

"Why you did that?" I said, and within seconds I heard several sets of feet stomping, voices shouting "Get out the way!" and keys jingling as several guard ran up the stairs into the room.

"Where they at?" a guard asked when he entered the room. He was breathing heavily.

"There," the guard who pressed his beeper said, pointing at us. "I caught them getting down."

"What?" said the other guard. "You mean you pressed your beeper 'cause they were fucking? What's wrong with you?" Then he said to Toby and me, "Strip."

As Toby and I took off our clothes, I tried to explain to him that the other guard had made a mistake, that I was only trying to get a good pair of jeans to wear to my grandmother's funeral. But the guard ignored my words as he watched Toby and me take off all our clothes.

While Toby and I stood naked in that room, lifting our bare feet up then down on the cold concrete floor, guards searched our clothes, and while prisoners walked past the room peeping in, the guard who had pressed his beeper sat at a desk writing out disciplinary reports. My write-up read:

I Sgt. Was making rounds and noticed a light on in Classroom Two. On entering I saw inmate Fabian Harper pulling his pants up and another inmate zipping his pants up quickly. Inmates placed in Admin Sec.

We were handcuffed and walked downstairs naked, past staring prisoners, out the door, and down to the hole. There a guard gave us red jumpsuits to put on, then placed us in separate cells.

In the hole all you do is sit on your bed and stare at the wall, the ceiling, the floor, and maybe count the drops of water coming out of the faucet and nothing else. There were no TV's, no radios or cards to help pass your time. Just an empty cell with a toilet and sheetless mattress for you to sleep on while you waited to be called before the disciplinary board guards. If you had a friend down the walk in one of the dorms, he would pay the prisoners working the hole feeding us to smuggle you in some candy, a bar of soap, notes, maybe even a few smokes. My only friend was locked up with me, so I didn't expect to be getting anything. However, that following morning the prisoner who brought me my tray told me that the prisoners who worked in the education building mopping the floors had told the guard Toby and me were upstairs having sex.

"The guard ain't know ya'll was up there until he told him," the prisoner said.

"How he looks?" I said, anxious to know.

"Kinda fat. Black. About my height," he said, standing straight up so I could get a good estimate. "And he gots a partial gray beard."

I thought, that's the guy I passed on the stairs. "Thanks," I told him.

I sat in that cell block thinking about the trouble that prisoner got me into, and I put in my mind that I was going to fight him. "Ride the motherfucker," I kept mumbling to myself, but I never got the chance. By the time I made it back on the wall, I learned that he had died.

I stayed in the hole three days before I was called before the DB guards. DB court was then what it is now. You were guilty before you walked in. Every prisoner knew this and usually tried to work out a deal for a less severe penalty with DB guards. If you tried to argue your write-up with the DB's, they gave you the harshest sentence they could impose for the rule infraction, which usually meant being sent back to a working cellblock. So most would rather plead guilty for the deal to not get transferred off of the walk.

This is what was said when I stepped into the DB room.

"I see you and another prisoner were having sex."

"Nossir."

"Ya'll weren't having sex?"

"Nossir."

Keep your answers short and simple was the rule among us prisoners. I could have told them that the write-up never said Toby and me were having sex, that the light was on in the room so it would have been stupid to try something like that, plus there was nothing found on me or Toby when the guard searched us: no grease, toilet paper, nothing that could be used for sex. But to say all that risked angering the DB's; they wanted me to plead guilty and get out of there fast.

"Didn't a guard catch you in a room with another prisoner?"

"Yessir."

"If you weren't having sex, why would the guard write you up for it then?"

There was no escape for this trap. The guards were always right. If I pointed out that the write-up didn't say I was having sex, the DB's would get angry, feeling like I was telling them how to do their job, and if I continued my denials, they would grow frustrated with me and send me back to the cellblock.

"That's what the guard wrote right here. Why would he just lie on you?"

"Not lie, misinterpret."

"You calling my guard a liar?"

"I'm just saying he mistook what he saw."

"Step out."

I walked out of the room so the DB's could confer and review my disciplinary record. I knew that I would be found guilty; I just hoped they would take my conduct record into consideration. Since my record was fairly decent, I didn't expect a harsh sentence. I heard one of the DB guards holler for me to step back into the room.

"The board notes your good conduct record; however, based on the credibility of the guard who wrote you up, the board finds you guilty and sentences you to a working cellblock. Good day."

I dropped my head and turned as I walked out of the room.

Chapter 6

I landed in B block just in time for the last yard call and was immediately approached by a tall black man who told me his name was Cotton Picker.

"Say, I'm your celly," he told me.

I could tell he was a homosexual. Though he was a big, squarely built man with an unshaven face, the sparkle in his eyes let me know he looked at me with motives.

"The guys in this block know not to mess with me," he said. I looked at the yard. Prisoners were walking around the dirt yard talking to each other while others stood by the basketball court watching the game. I noticed one of the prisoners playing was in C block when I first came to prison. He continued, "They know I look out for my cellys, so no one will mess with you."

I shrugged my shoulders; then out of nowhere appeared a slender black man,

"Say, you play football tickets?"

"I don't have no Camels to bet with," I said.

"You can play and pay later."

I didn't want to say that I didn't know how to play tickets; that would have been an indicator that I was fairly naïve to the prison way of life, so I made up an excuse I thought was good.

"I don't believe in betting on my ass," I told him.

"Maybe you—-" Cotton Picker butted in. "He said he don't play, so leave him alone."

The prisoner gave Cotton Picker a begrudging stare, but he walked off.

"He's a bitch," Cotton Picker said. "Everybody knows about him but him." Then he invited me to walk around the yard. As we walked, he told me who were the hard hitters in the block, a who's who list, then he told me how the block was run. And though I listened, I noticed how he tried to read my expression every time he said, "That's an undercover bulldogger," or "He's a rat," each time we walked past another prisoner.

That night in our cell a prisoner working our tier brought us our supper trays: field squash, black-eyed peas spread on top of white rice, with a piece of chocolate cake. Cotton Picker took his cake off his tray and began wrapping it in his toilet paper wrapper.

"I'm gonna save this for you to eat tonight," he said.

"I don't want it," I told him.

"I ain't gonna eat it."

"I don't eat at night."

Cotton Picker stared at me for a long second, then tossed the wrapped up cake into the toilet.

"Oh well," he said, "a good piece of cake gone."

After we ate, we watched TV and waited for the guard to open our cell door for shower. A re-run of *Good Times* was playing on the TV. We laughed at JJ and made comments about the memories the show brought back. We did this often; old movies and songs on the radio often triggered a memory, and our minds were momentarily thrown back to a place when our lives were simpler, less burdensome: when we had laughed with messy mouths of chocolate, grinned as we jumped rope, and smiled while we waited patiently for the photographer to snap our prom picture.

Our cell door opened for us to go take a shower. We walked to the front of the tier to the first cell that had been converted to a two-man shower. Once we stepped inside, the block guard closed the shower door behind us. That shower was too small for two naked men. There were only two shower heads. Unless we stood directly under them, the water would not hit our bodies, and so we wouldn't bump into each other, we took turns turning our backs, then our faces to the showers. As we showered, Cotton Picker didn't say a word to me, though occasionally I caught him from the corner of my eye glancing at my butt every time he turned around to rinse the soap off his back, and I would cut my eyes down to him every so often to make sure he didn't have a hard on.

After we showered, we went back to our cell and hung our wet clothes that we washed in the shower on a line we had made out of torn pieces of sheet that we tied together to stretch from the back of the cell to the front. One end we threaded through the air vent holes at the back of the cell, stretching the sheet to the top of the front cell bars where we tied the two ends together. While I was hanging up my socks, t-shirt, then towel, Cotton Picker asked me what I thought about God. I figured he asked the question because of the many religious books he saw I had in my locker box.

"I believe in him," I said.

"Do you really?" he asked.

That was the first time I ever felt a conviction in a question. I have to say that it lit the spirit in me to get serious about knowing God. Though I grew up in church and always felt a tug in my heart to proclaim God's word, I always ignored that nudging. But Cotton Picker's question, it jarred me. It made the nerves in my stomach jump. But I didn't want him to know the impact of his simple questions, so I quickly answered, "Yep, I do."

"I don't believe in all that," Cotton Picker told me. I understood. The pressure of life sentences breeds anger and hate in men's hearts. Religion in prison operates more as a pressure release valve than as a truly soul-changing experience. It is psychological therapy, nothing more. A man in prison wants to be free. Religion provides a simple word, "Hope." Hope that God will look from his heavenly throne and see the tears of hurt and the looks of frustration and bless us with our freedom. Not a day goes by that a prisoner doesn't hope for that day when he will be reunited with his family, playing with his children, and living out his life without restraint. But incarceration makes him confront daily his physical limitations, and the pain of this reality drives a prisoner to church to ask God for his physical deliverance. This is what any man doing a long sentence truly prays for. In prisoner-led services each prayer, each sermon, each song is underlined with a call for freedom. And prisoners will shout, clap, and sing to God, hoping that their praises will invoke him to grant them their freedom. But when their call is not answered, eventually, over time, some prisoners will slowly stop attending religious services, distancing themselves from those churchgoer zealots and become hostile and angry at God.

Over the next few weeks Cotton Picker's and my schedules were pretty routine. We went to work, came in to eat, talked while we waited to shower, and went to sleep. Occasionally we played chess or watched TV. Sometimes I read my books. Then one night as we were getting our things ready for the shower, he asked me why I was in the block.

"You never told me," he said, "and I was just wondering." Cotton Picker had given me enough hints that he was homosexual; therefore, I knew he would not believe that I was only trying to change pants with Toby. Any explanation I gave him I knew would be interpreted by him as a cover, so I lied.

"Man, some guard in the education building wrote me up for not having my pass signed," I said. "He said I was in an unauthorized area. And you know D.B.; if you don't take their deal, they slam you. That's what they done to me, sent me to the blocks."

He gave me a blank stare, then said, "Yeah, they fucked me over too."

His look made me nervous. I was trying to read what he was thinking, and as soon as the words, "I heard you was in the education building bulldogging with some white boy," came out of his mouth, I knew I was in trouble. I sat on the toilet looking at him, my mind quickly searching for an appropriate response. Then I settled on one.

"Whoever told you that bullshit lied to you," I said, my face frowning for added emphasis.

"Look, can we bulldog?" he said.

"I'm not into that shit."

"They said you only let white boys fuck you."

"What? Man, if you believe that stuff, don't talk to me no more," and I stood to climb into my bed when Cotton Picker lunged, smashing his fist into my temple. My foot slipped from the toilet seat and I fell backward into the cell wall. Dazed, I swung wild, connecting with his jaw. He grabbed me around the waist twisting and pulling at me, trying to wrestle me to the ground. But I kept my back pressed against the cell wall and threw short jabs to his head and body. He countered with a few licks of his own. To win a cell fight, one has to have a greater will to survive. Fights are as much about instinct as they are about skill. Any instantaneous thought that comes to your mind and will help you gain the advantage, you use. And at one point I had a perfect shot at his eyeballs. I could have grabbed the ink pen that was on my bed and stabbed it into one of his eyes. But a thought went through my mind. Strangely, I knew he didn't want to hurt me. He was only fighting as hard as I was because I had shocked him by fighting back. When I realized this, I said low, "You'll have to kill me," and he let me go.

"We can't live together," he said, stepping back and taking in deep breaths.

"I ain't going nowhere," I said.

There may be some who have never lived behind prison walls that will question the rationale of my response. However, your time in prison is as easy or hard as your rep is, and your prison rep is built off of how you respond in moments of adversity. In prison there is no such thing as a good retreat. You either stand or wimp out; it's that simple. The stand is what's important. It doesn't matter if you win, lose, or draw, you just better stand. If I had voluntarily left the cell after our fight, word would get around prison that I had "checked out," a term meaning that I left under duress, and that only would make my stay in prison more difficult. Better to be known as a bulldogger that will fight than a punk who is scared.

"You're the one who's leaving," I told him, then socked him in his mouth and he fell back into the cell door.

We began another series of throwing wild punches, grabbing, wrestling, and choking each other. Suddenly, I heard, "Break it up!" but I ignored it and continued to sneak in short jabs as Cotton Picker held me around my waist.

"Open it up!" the voice hollered. I heard the electronic sound of the door, then the pop, and as the cell door slid back, I was grabbed in a chokehold from behind and pulled out of the cell by the cellblock guard.

"Close it!" he hollered down to his co-worker, and the cell door closed.

I came out of that fight with a busted lip, swollen eyes, a cracked tooth, and a swollen jaw, and when I stood before the DB officers, they looked at me and said, "Since you like to fight, we're sending you to Camp D Raven working cellblock."

Chapter 7

Camp D Raven: "Dodge City" was what we prisoners called it back then. Raven was the most feared cellblock on Angola Farm. The ambulance, which we called the "meat wagon," rolled daily to pick up a prisoner who had been stabbed, beaten, hit in the head with a brick, locks, or a field tool. For five prisoners who died by the hand of another prisoner, three of them were killed at Camp D. Guards were also killed there. You were worked to death at Raven, fed like dogs, and guards talked to you like you were nothing. The old guards used to say that such treatment was deserved since the prisoners who were sent to Raven were animals. I remember one time I was standing with my back against the wall watching a card game when a prisoner walked up behind one of the prisoners and stabbed him in the neck with a rusted nail, leaving him unconscious. Those of us who were around walked casually away, leaving the unconscious prisoner on the ground for the guards to find him. But, strangely, for all of the trouble Raven prisoners got into, my times back there were easy. I never had a slight argument. But I do remember my first time back there.

Just entering Camp D was depressing. The transport van drove through a set of massive double gates that electronically slid open, then closed slowly behind the van, cutting you off from the rest of the prison. The van paused as a second set of double gates slid back, the van drove through, and I turned to watch as those gates slowly closed.

The van stopped in front of a small gate that opened to a walkway. I immediately noticed that no one was around. It was quiet. The only noise I heard was the transport guard telling me to watch my step as I got out of the van.

When I finally made it to the cellblock, a guard inside unlocked the door, and I walked in. I stepped into a lobby bustling with activity. I had arrived just in time for lunch. In the lobby were two prisoners in prison blues with white paper caps on their heads standing behind a metal steam table scraping mashed potatoes from the bottoms of the pans with big metal spoons, then hitting the spoons against the plastic trays. Four different prisoners hurried back and forth past me yelling, "I need four more!" at the prisoners fixing the trays and picking the food up. They hurried to carry them down the tiers to the cells. The noise of *The Young and the Restless* blared from TV's, and prisoners hollered from their cells, "Bring me my juice!" out at the lobby.

I stood there shackled and handcuffed while the two guards sat at their desk; one was eating while the other was writing in the log book. After he finished writing, he got up, took the shackles and handcuffs off me, then told me, "Cell 2." As I walked into the tier, prisoners stuck small pieces of mirrors they had glued to pencils or to the back of their tooth brushes to see who I was. This made me uneasy, for I wondered what they had heard, what they had been thinking. As the cell door opened, I was relieved to find the cell empty.

Since I was in the cell first, I had my choice of the upper or lower bunk. Most prisoners hated climbing up and jumping down, therefore preferring the lower bunk, but I had found the upper bunk warmer. During summer months I simply tossed my mat on the floor and slept. Though I was relieved to be in the cell all by myself, I knew I wouldn't be alone long. Soon my door would open and another prisoner would walked in carrying his bundles of clothes. When, you never knew. The guards never gave you a choice of cellmates. When a new prisoner arrived, you could only hope that the prisoner wouldn't be sent in your cell, but that hope was usually dashed.

Since I was going to be in the cell with someone, I rehearsed in my mind the convict ethic of moving into another prisoner's cell. If he wasn't there when I moved in, I would put my bundle on the floor, sit on the toilet seat, and wait for him to come back. Don't touch his things, I told myself. Instead, sit there reading his character from the way he has kept his cell and his things. Is his bed neatly made, or does he have wrinkles in his sheets? Is the floor swept clean? Does the toilet have a ring in it? Do his shoes have mud on their soles? Does he have a pile of legal papers stacked in the corner or books lined up on the empty bunk? I would sit there anxious to see who I would be sleeping under or on top of. Usually the type of prisoner who walked through the cell door would be a large black whose skin glistened with sweat from working in the fields and stunk, or a white who was dusty like a cowboy and smelled like he had been sleeping in a barn, his beard not having been shaved in months and his stringy hair tangled up like wire on his head, or a homosexual who at night walked around the cell in a long white t-shirt and a pair of homemade panties and stood at the bars grinning and flirting with the different men that walked past the cell.

When cellying with someone you are getting along with, you wanted to keep him, so you hoped he didn't ride out or go to the hole. Out in the yard you helped him with his work if you saw him struggling, you kept your ears open for plotters, and you stood up with him when the cell door opened for yard call to make sure no one ran in the cell on him because to let that happen was disrespecting you. And when the guard hollered down the tier, "Work Call!" and the cell doors slammed back, you watched men as they stepped out of their cells and lined the wall, making sure no one snuck up on him. If your celly did go the hole and was transferred, you hoped for a few days alone. You could take a crap in peace and shower by yourself. Each of these days alone is cherished because you know it will be long before you have another. One afternoon you come in from work and there he is, his bundle yet unpacked, waiting to meet you.

I had some interesting cellys during my time spent at Raven. All one did was sit on his locker box writing letters to his girlfriend. On canteen day he would spend all of his money on legal pads, pens, and stamps. He sat on his box for hours listening to his headphone radio, writing to these pictures he had spread over his bed. The pictures were of his girlfriend at a swimming pool, in her back yard, or smiling sitting on a sofa. And though he would never receive a response from her, he diligently wrote pages to her each night. Then one day while talking to his mother on the phone, he had her call his girlfriend using the three-way phone service. To his surprise, some man answered the phone and told him never to call there again. I remember him saying he heard a baby crying in the background. That night, he tore up all her pictures and flushed them down the toilet.

I had another celly who snored and ground his teeth during the night. I would jump down out of my bed and tap the rail of his bunk to get him to roll over. Soon this stopped working and I learned to sleep through the noise. If the noise he made while he was asleep wasn't enough, he would fart and the odor floated up into my nose and smelled so bad that I had to open my mouth to breathe.

One of my cellys liked to talk a lot. He told me about every girl-friend he had had and every crime he had committed. Everything he did earned him thousands. He had robbed a store for thousands, made thousands selling drugs, pimped his girls for thousands. As I listened to him, I thought to myself, "With all the thousands he collected, why did he go to trial with a court appointed attorney?" I realized he just needed someone to talk to, and so I would lie in my bed and let him tell me his stories while my mind drifted to my family or court, and at intervals my senses would alert me to give an appropriate response like "Really?"

I had another celly who was quiet as long as he had something to smoke. Because he didn't have any money to buy cigarettes out of the canteen, he would pick the butts off the rec yard and ask prisoners on the tier for theirs. I would carefully watch him tear open the paper of the butts so as not to lose a tobacco string, then re-roll the tobacco in a piece of toilet paper wrapper or in a page torn from the Bible. Those cigarettes would smell like wood burning, and he coughed terribly with each pull he took. He was later diagnosed with TB. He wondered how. "Must've been from smoking those re-rolled butts," was what the nurse who brought his meds to the cell told him.

One of my cellys, all he did was complain. He complained about the food, about work, about the guards. I hated talking to him because he was sure to find something in our conversation to complain about. His favorite complaint was against our neighbors, how they were homosexuals.

"Listen to them over there," he would say, "with all that laughing and playing." Tonight they goin' to be jumpin' in each other's ass."

"What they're doing, what has that to do with you?" I would tell him. "They in their cell."

He'd look at me and say, "God needs to kill them all."

Though I didn't agree with my neighbors' lifestyle, I understood it. In doing time, I have learned that the only loyalty that exists behind these walls is between lovers. All other associations have limitations, but not two men in love. Only they, I have seen, will sacrifice their personal needs to ensure that the other will have those things he desires. They show a genuine concern when one of them is hurting and an untiring aid when one of them is sick. They will likely put their lives on the line to protect each other. Outside the bonds of two lovers it is hard to find the same expression between prisoners. Those who will show some of the same affection toward another prisoner generally do so for their own hidden purposes. It is different with lovers, however; they will be back by each other's side no matter how grave the circumstances. They are each other's support, and to separate them is to invoke their wrath. Their love for each other is stronger than family blood. I have witnessed a father having his son as his whore and cousins screwing each other, but the man in love with another man will not abuse, use, mistreat, or neglect his companion. They may fight, as seemingly all couples do, but they will make up. Unlike family members that grew up under the same roof in prison, two men who have grown up cities apart will display a true family compassion. And that was the essence that my complaining celly missed. He wondered how two men could develop such a loving relationship. Because there is nothing to do at Raven but work and all you see are the same prisoners, it gets boring back there quickly, and you find yourself more and more reflecting on your life wasting away behind bars. Such thoughts lead to mixed feelings of vengeance and discontent. But the realization that you have no one that will help you, not even your family, weighs you down. You begin to think all is lost. You want to just give up, end it all, or pray for death to take you to end the emotional suffering of hopelessness and loneliness that confronts you every day you wake up. To say that I have not had such thoughts would not be true.

I can recall one night when those demons of loneliness were riding me. Everyone on the tier was asleep. It was raining. I lay awake listening to the echoes of men's snores through the faint sounds of thunderclaps. I thought about my childhood, my mind flooding with memories of happier times. I saw my sister laughing, playing on the floor with her dolls, my mother diving into my bed while I was asleep, tickling me until I woke up. There was my grandmother, smiling and crying the day I was baptized at Paradise Baptist Church. And my mind seemed to move slowly past scenes of family outings when my mother took us to the park, skating rink, and to Chucky Cheese so I could jump in the cage of blue, yellow, and red balls. I lay there feeling like I was forgotten, written off, so there was no one I existed for. My life was nothing behind bars, I told myself in anger. Sniffling, I stood up with my sheet and went to the cell bars when suddenly there were loud claps of thunder, and lightning flashed through the window outside my cell. I looked up and saw my mother's face silhouetted on the glass. But as quickly as the lightning had flashed, she was gone, covered up by the darkness. And it was again quiet, except for the men's snores. I stood at the bars looking at the dark window. There's no person I have ever felt closer to than my mother. I believe God revealed her face to me at that time to let me know I was not forgotten. I smiled, went back to my bed and lay down.

Besides having to put up with cellmates at Raven, there was the field.

The line pusher worked our mouths dry cutting ditches of tall grass, throwing bales of hay, or chopping wood. In the field, we tried not to think about the work we were doing and so distracted our minds by talking, cracking jokes, or reciting rap lyrics to each other. Occasionally, during the course of a work day something would happen to provide a momentary excitement. I can remember one summer morning, standing in line with the other prisoners, waiting for my friends Adrian Brown and Brandon Stein. A crowd of prisoners had walked past me, and I started to wonder if they were standing at the back of the line.

"There you are," I said. "I thought I was going to have to come back and look for you."

Adrian lifted his hoe onto his shoulder, then tilted his head at Stein. He was rubbing his finders across blades trying to find a sharp one.

Stein grinned. "I bet I won't be struggling if we cut grass today."

We were standing in our little group talking when the line pusher who was in charge of working us in the field came riding up on his horse. The horse's dry smell made me turn my lip up as the line pusher rode past us. I noticed there were jagged lines of sweat running down the horse's side from underneath the saddle, and I knew the

August heat was going to make my morning aggravating.

When the line pusher made it to the front of the line, he raised his voice above ours. "Line up!" he hollered.

Stein got next to me and Adrian got behind us next to another prisoner. After we all were paired off, our line pusher yelled out, "Walk it!"

The line started to move and we fell in step with each other, following the prisoners in front of us walking to the field where we would work. I had met Adrian and Stein down the walk, having introduced them to each other while picking yellow squash one day. We had been friends ever since.

"So," I said, as we walked down a dirt and gravel road. Our steps smashing in the rocks and dirt sounded like Grape Nuts cereal being chewed. "What you think our line pusher will have us doing today?"

"Don't know," Adrian said. He squinted his eyed to look up at the clear sky. "I hope it ain't a lot, though."

"He'll probably have us doing what we've been doing the last two days," Stein said. "Picking purple hull peas."

"I hope not," I said. "My back still aches from all that bending over yesterday."

"Then why are we toting these tools?" Adrian asked, wiping sweat away from his forehead with his thumb. The bright sun was slowly pushing over our heads, and its rays beaming directly down on us felt like a hot oven. He wiped his thumb dry on his pants leg. "Having us carry these hoes all the way out here just to stack them in a pile don't make sense."

"I know," I said, pinching my t-shirt away from my chest. "But you know they always want us to carry a tool even if we don't use it. That's their little way of making us tired while we walk," and we walked at a hyper pace that warm morning down the stretch of road. The sun seemed to follow us, its heat burning the back of our necks. I felt warm beads of sweat running down my back, and I took in big breaths as I pushed myself to keep close to the man in front of me.

We had been walking for thirty minutes when I finally asked, "Where are we going?" as we turned off the road down a stretch of trail, then cut through a grassy field. Then I saw where we were headed. It was another field of purple hull peas. We walked to the front of the field and stopped.

"Alright you convicts," the line pusher said, slowly riding his horse down beside us.

" I want the grass scraped from around the plants and out of the gutters of the rows. Don't break the plants or you will pay for them and I will send you to the hole. Then pull all your loose grass to the back of the field and spread it out. Don't leave none of your grass piled up. Stop at the water buckets in the middle of the field. You got fifteen minutes to make it to them. Now get to work."

There were 160 quarter mile rows I counted, just enough for every man in our line to work. Prisoners began to walk to rows they had visually selected. Of course, they chose rows that didn't have much grass on them.

Stein looked at me, pointing at his hoe, and smiled. "I told you," he said, before starting to chop at the grass in the gutter of the row he stood on.

I looked out at the field, shaking my head. The field of purple hull peas had not been cared for. The sun had turned their bright purple shells brown and dried the peas inside to hard, small, pebbles. Bugs had eaten holes in the black, brown, and green withered leaves. And patches of tall, thorny weeds had grown between each plant of peas and in the rows' gutters. I wondered how our line pushers expected us not to break the plants when wild vines had grown up from the ground, twisting themselves around the peas' stalks and stems.

"Damn." I took the hoe from my shoulder and started to cut the grass.

"This ground is hard," Stein told himself. He was working on the row next to me. To one side, two prisoners chatted together as they worked to pull a pile of grass backwards with their hoes. On the other side of us, a prisoner quietly chopped at the grass by himself while another prisoner started chopping grass around the water buckets. They would meet in the middle of the row.

"Yeah," I answered Stein. "They need to plow this whole field up, instead of trying to save it so they can feed us this crap," I said, chopping away at the weeds at a steady pace. The sun gave me no relief as I worked. It hung over me shining bright in the blue sky. Its heat burned my naked arms as sweat ran down my forehead. I grunted while beating my hoe against the hard dirt, trying to get under the roots of the weeds.

Stein and I finally made it to the water buckets.

"I'm glad we're not last," I said, propping my hoe's handle under my arm. There were a few prisoners still working.

"You got five minutes!" our line pusher hollered from his saddle.

We stood by the water buckets with a few other prisoners, catching our breath and watching the other prisoners work. They started moving their hoes faster, realizing that the fifteen minutes the line pusher had given them to be finished was nearly up.

While I stood with Stein looking at those prisoners cut down the grass in their rows, he pulled from his back pocket a folded white envelope wrapped in plastic. "I got this from court yesterday," he said, passing me a sheet of paper that he pulled from the envelope. "It's the court's ruling on my post-conviction appeal."

"What did they say?"

"They denied me," he said. "But look at why they denied me He pointed to a paragraph at the bottom of the page.

Though your claim has constitutional merit, because you failed to submit your appeal within the two year period, your appeal is therefore procedurally barred under Louisiana Code of Criminal Procedure 930.8 For these reasons assigned, your appeal for post-conviction relief is denied.

I shook my head, handing the paper back to Stein. "That's cold."

"I know," he said. He took the paper, folded it, then stuffed it back inside the envelope.

"I mean, they gave me two years to get my claim into court, but they take eighteen months getting my court papers to me. Since I ain't go to law school, what they expected me to do in six months." He stuffed the envelope down into his pocket. "I tell you this, I'm not giving up. If they think—" A scream cut him off and snatched my head around. I looked straight out over the field and saw a small bunch of prisoners running towards us. I clutched my hoe.

"Kill it!" I heard a prisoner shout, running for us, holding his hoe in the air. Kill it!"

I heard something coming up behind me, thrump, thrumping against the hard dirt. It was the line pusher riding up, then past me into the crowd of running prisoners.

"Stop running!" he screamed.

The prisoners stopped.

"Kill it!" one of them shouted, looking at the ground. Anger boiled inside of me as I stared at his back as he rode away.

I followed his eyes and saw what all of them were after, a tiny grass snake.

"Leave that snake alone," the line pusher shouted. "Get back to work."

Slowly, the prisoners started walking back to their rows, some mumbling to themselves, a few holding conversations with each other. I was still standing next to the water buckets watching the prisoners walk away when—

"You!" the line pusher snapped.

I looked up into his face. "Yessir," I said.

"I said get back to work,"

"But I'm...."

"I don't want to hear what you got to say," he said. "I said go back to work or you can go to the hole."

There was no use trying to reason with him. I clutched my hoe and began to chop at the grass in the space I was standing in. The line pusher watched me a few minutes before turning his horse's head and went back toward the front of the field. Anger boiled inside of me as I stared at his back as he rode away. "I'll be glad when this half is over with," I mumbled, cutting the grass.

The prisoners running after that snake was not unusual. There was always a prisoner chasing something: a turtle, a field mouse, a rabbit. Sometimes, however, we were chased after by ground hornets, bats, and even coons. Though these times gave us much excitement and amusement, I want to be clear, none of us enjoyed working in the fields. We worked in all types of weather. It never got too hot for us to go out to work, and it seemed the cold weather always hovered just above freezing, warm enough for a line pusher to take us out in the fields. It had to rain extremely hard for us to be called out of the fields. Light to moderate downpours we worked in. I have come in many days with my clothes drenched from the rain.

Soon you get tired of living in the blocks. The limited space and sameness grinds at you, and you begin to miss the prisoners you met in population, the greater feel of freedom that comes with being housed in a dorm, and you were ready to go back. In the block, we never knew how long we had to be there. Based on why we were sent to the block, we could estimate how much time we had to serve before the re-class board decided to re-assign us back into population. We had our own body of wisdom that, if we stayed write-up free, when the board came around in 90 days, it would grant us leave. So we bore the field work, the heat, the line pushers' yelling and insults, and we completed 90 days without a write-up, becoming eligible to go before the re-class board for consideration back into population.

As the day for re-class approached, we would start gathering in small huddles to exchange stories to tell the board members. The board members knew we would say and promise anything just to get them to re-assign us. To make no excuses, admit our wrong, act remorseful, and pretend to agree with their advice was the plan we settled on.

I walked before the re-class board members confident that they would classify me back to population. I had done my ninety days in the field without a write-up, I hadn't caused any problems for the block guards, and I got along with my celly. I stood before the board members, only to return to my cell feeling weak, blankheaded, empty. There I read the paper they had handed me as if the words written on it would be different from what they told me.

Decision by the Board: Denied

Reason: Board Discretion

Another 90 days—at least another 90 days—of putting up with the line pusher, smelling my cell's stinky socks, and avoiding those prisoners who lived to start trouble with other prisoners.

The next morning at Work Call I saw one of the Board members talking to the block guard in the lobby, and I walked up to him.

"Say, classification, why ya'll denied me on the Board?"

"What you're in for?"

"I was hit with a twenty-one."

"That's all. Well, I'll put you on the special Board in thirty days."

That's what they always said. The re-class board members were just like prisoners. They would say anything to get you out of their face.

But you're never dejected for long. Within days you start to think about the next board, when you will have strengthened your chances— you will have done another 90 write-up free. That's one thing re-class can not easily overlook, the amount of time you have gone without catching another write-up. So you begin your journey. You go to work when your cell door rolls back, and as each day passes, your confidence increases that you will make the next board. There are the right phrases or words that always work, if only you can figure out what they are. Your mind focuses on this. You carefully analyze each reason others made the board. You break down their words, trying to discover the secret code, and then it is re-class day again.

You sit in your cell listening to the tables being dragged to the front of the tier. Large plastic boxes containing files slam down on the floor.

Hearings never start until after noon chow, but the block guards had us up and working before breakfast. One of the guards walks down the tier raking a stick across our cell bars, yelling for us to get ready to see the Board. "Board Day, Board Day," he repeats as he walks down, then back up the tier, raking on the bars. The guards don't send us out to work that morning. They'll let you out of your cell to shower if you wish. You comb your hair and put on your best clothes. You do all of this, hoping your clean appearance will help convince the board members that you are ready for population.

As you sit in your cell waiting, you go over what to say to their questions. You try not to get a response settled in your mind because you don't want to sound rehearsed. "Take deep breaths, look them straight in the eye," you tell yourself. Then you hear the lobby door open and you begin to get nervous. You listen to the men's and women's voices talking loud. Is this a sign? They appear to be in a good mood. And then the first door rolls open.

You stand at the bars trying to read the face of each prisoner who returns from the Board. Many are white-faced, a few visibly angry, others shake their heads. Someone who is waiting will always ask:

"Really, man, what's their mood like?"

"Fucked up."

"They let you talk?"

"No."

Such a response never gave any of us much hope. The board had a pattern. When they didn't let anyone say anything, that meant they had already let a lot of prisoners go from other blocks, so you knew your chances of being released were cut by 99%. But you still held out that slim chance that you would get lucky. And that kept you standing at the bars waiting in anticipation.

My door popped and it slid back. I stepped out of my cell and walked up the tier. I stood before the board members. One of them stared at me, another was writing, and the third asked, "What's your number?"

"33 63 74."

He reached into the box next to him, pulling from it a thick green folder—my file. He opened it and there was silence as he read over the write-up that sent me to the block. Then he began to flip back a few pages, looking over other write-ups. Optimism started to die seeing that. For it was at that point the last time that I was handed a paper reading "Denied." He then slid my file to the next board member for her to look over as he asked me, "You feel you're ready for population?"

"He asked me a question!" I thought. "There is a chance." I answered him in the sincerest voice possible.

"Yessir."

"You feel you will come back to the block if we let you go?" the woman asked.

I wanted to tell her she knew that we got written up on the smallest thing. Most of the write-ups we received were accusations by guards who had a beef with you, or because you didn't rat, or because he was just an asshole. And if we didn't play along with DB's little games, they sent us to the block. Even the Board now was a game, a charade to get me to grovel. In fact, that was why I was in the block—for bucking the program of their well-trained system of things. For not begging.

And as long as I know I'm right, I will continue to reject those normal ways of how things are done in this prison. Will I return to the block? Probably so. But, of course, I did not tell her any of this. Instead I answered politely, "No ma'am. If you give me the chance, I won't be coming back."

She looked at me, then wrote on a piece of paper and slid it to the other members of the Board to sign. She then handed it to me.

"Keep up the good work," she said.

Denied again. Another 90 days. I began thinking that maybe I should push my locker boxes out of my cell and go to the hole so I could get transferred to another camp's block where I might have a chance of getting released by their board. But this idea faded as I realized that I would have to do at least six months there before any of these boards would consider letting me go. So, instead, I fixed my mind on doing another 90 days.

But when I next heard those tables slide across the floor again, it turned out that I got lucky, as a few of us did, and was released back into general population.

Chapter 8

I was transferred back down the walk to the prison's main compound. Many of the same prisoners were still there. That's one thing I have learned over the years about this place: not a lot of older prisoners move around much. They are settled. They call it convicting, learning how to do time. The guards, however, call it adjusting. I call it accepting their lowly status.

This time on the walk, I told myself, I wasn't going to hang around anyone; I would be a loner. But I have been here long enough to know that even keeping to yourself upsets some prisoners, so I had decided to employ some simple psychology to keep down hostilities. Whenever I saw a prisoner walking down the walkway, I hoped he would look the other way or pass me without speaking. But because I knew that was wishful thinking, as we got closer to one another, for the purpose of appearing civil, I would give a smiling hello, but deep down I hated him. I knew that no sooner had he left my sight, he would be huddled in a group with other prisoners plotting on someone, possibly me. But I found my tactic more effective in blunting trouble than the brute methods I used in the past—fighting and trading insult for insult.

But it's very hard to be alone, to not want to talk with someone. All life requires some communication of sorts, and I found myself desiring some form of socialization. So I started attending church services and Bible studies. I avoided the services that were held by prisoners. I didn't trust any of them. Too often I saw many of the prison ministers just wanting to boast that they had a following. I decided instead on fellowship with churches that came in the prison to hold services, "people from the outside" we called them. They were safe. I didn't know them, they didn't know me, and I didn't have to worry about an attachment, yet I could socialize. It fit fine.

And yet, as weeks drifted to months, my emptiness increased. I felt abandoned, and my mind kept telling me that I was growing old in here. By this time I had gotten a job working as a clerk for the literacy program, and I tried not to think about my life just sitting and wasting, and so occupied my time going back and forth to work, attending church, or exercising. But none of that brought me comfort. No matter how hard I tried to distract my mind from the inside and submerge it with activities of this small world, I couldn't. I knew there existed a bigger world beyond these walls that I wanted to be a part of, and my soul yearned to escape the wretchedness I live in. This desire eats at you, and soon you start to doubt the God the preachers told you about. You grow quiet, distant.

The frightening aspect that I may die here confronted me one day as I was walking along the walk headed for lunch. I was walking in a single line with other prisoners going to the kitchen when I saw a fellow in a wheel chair for the first time. It was a clear, hot autumn afternoon, and he was sitting on the opposite side of the walkway that connected our dormitories. I came out of my dorm walking fast because I wanted to be among the first served my meal instead of having to stand in a long line of waiting prisoners. I hardly paid attention to him that first time, except for noticing from the corner of my eye his raising his head to look at me just as I was passing him. If he had wanted someone to push him, why hadn't he stopped one of the other prisoners as they passed?

I kept walking.

The next afternoon as I came down the walkway, I saw him again sitting in the same place. Without giving any thought to it, I stepped out of the line of flowing prisoners directly to his path. As I walked closer to him, up came his head again with precision.

There was something about his eyes' empty stare that made me feel uneasy. But as I was deciding not to push him, I walked up to his wheelchair, reached my hands out, and firmly gripped hold of its back handles.

He didn't utter a word as I gripped his wheelchair handles. He just sat straight with his hands clasped in his lap waiting for me to begin pushing. But as I squeezed the handles ready to push him into the line of moving prisoners, he twisted his neck to look up at me. He had the most depressing eyes I had ever seen.

"I a dieter," he said. The smell of his bad breath, having the odor of rotten teeth, angered me.

I nodded, turning my head slightly away. "I'll push you up to the window," I told him. Even the sight of his face angered me. His eyes still had white mucus from sleep buried in their corners and between the folds of the wrinkles of his forehead were thin lines of dirt. If it had been early in the morning I could have understood his appearance, but it was the afternoon, so there was no excuse for his filthy face. And his clothes. His blue shirt was wrinkled and stained with blots of coffee. The jeans he wore had holes in the knees and the thighs were faded white. Even the pockets were stained brown from sliding his hands in and out of them. He must have been confined to his wheelchair for a long time judging from his boney arms, flat chest, and skinny legs. But even in a wheelchair he could keep himself clean, I thought. Maybe that's why no one pushed him.

I spotted an opening in the line of prisoners and hurried to push him into it. He sat with his back straight, saying nothing, seemingly unconcerned with the speed at which I pushed him.

Now that I had us in the line, I slowed down slightly when he started coughing. Hearing him wheeze as he coughed, I began to feel bad for having an unreasoned disdain for him. But I quickly reminded myself that even bums take the time to bathe their bodies and change their clothes. "He's just being lazy," I thought.

I then made a polite effort at conversation. "I've never seen you before. You just got here?"

He said nothing. I knew he heard me; I had seen his head move. I tried again. This time I raised my voice.

"You just got to Angola?"

This time he slowly shook his head, then said, "No. I've been here 33 years." His voice was low, I barely heard him. He added, "They had me living on the hospital ward." He then let out a hard, gagging cough.

I turned my head away. "Man, what's wrong with you?" I asked frowning. My voice was sharp, almost hostile.

He let out a low, but audible, "Cancer." He paused as if trying to decide whether to say more, then added, "I came on the walk to die."

These words struck me. I know that death will eventually catch up to us all, but dying in prison is a fate no prisoner hopes will happen to him. No prisoner wants to die in Angola, and the reality of it happening to the man I was pushing brought to mind my worst fear.

As prisoners, we spend our days, sometimes nights, fantasizing about being free. We talk to one another about how, when we get out, we are going to make up for lost time, how we are going to use the skills we learned to apologize for the hurt we caused our families, and the many great things we will accomplish. But when keeping up with the days of the week gradually stops mattering, and you stop counting the number of gray strings growing in your hair, those wishful thoughts of freedom become fainter in your mind. And the reality that you may never see the outside world again presses closer to the front of your daily thoughts. Many prisoners hope they will leave Angola, but most do not. Most will grow old and die here. I was jailed at sixteen, so you know I don't want to die here, but I might, and that scares me.

For the prisoners who die in Angola, if no one comes to get their body, a funeral service will be held for them by prisoners. The bodies are carried to their graves in the prison's old graveyard, Point Lookout, in a black wooden hearse carriage pulled slowly by two white horses as prisoners walk behind singing, "I'm fr-ee, I'm fr-ee, Thank God, I'm fr-ee."

At the graveside the prisoner's wooden casket is gingerly lowered into the ground. A prisoner preacher will deliver his eulogy. The irony for many prisoners, who after enduring decades of laboring hard in exhausting heat and praying to God for freedom, is that he is laid to rest in a grassy plain a half mile from the front gate that he spent years dreaming to reach.

A whistle blew the next morning. From my book, I looked out my dormitory's window at the fenced in area where I gathered with the other prisoners to be checked out for work. There were little diamond shaped holes and silver coating that even in the early morning darkness were bright and sparkled through the dew that hung from their metal exterior.

I had developed a routine of looking out every morning at the bullpen to see if there would be a call for work. And each morning I saw, as the fine beams of moonlight broke across the ground, prisoners riding on the line pushers' horses toward the pen's front gate and guards walking out to meet them. Often I stayed there hoping my line pusher stayed home, and I would be spared the morning sun and afternoon heat of the field.

But as surely as I tried to fool myself, even as I attempted to do it, lie to myself that I wasn't going out to the fields, another whistle blew strong and loud—that was the whistle for work, long hours of working in the vegetable fields.

Slowly, I reached for my towel that hung on my bed, and rubbing my eyes, I staggered to the restroom where the prisoners' laughing and talking loud jarred the fuzzy feeling I had in my brain. I thought about the man in the wheelchair as I splashed water on my face and stared into the metal mirror thinking, "What kind of work will we do in the field today? What kind of work? What kind of work?"

It was another hot, clear morning in Angola prison. No air blew against my face as I stepped down the two concrete steps that led to the recreation yard; the blades of grass stood stiff, and I felt the warm sun-beams on my arm. I pinched my t-shirt off of my chest. "Pheww. Another hot one."

I looked toward the bullpen and saw it slowly crowding with pris-oners. I really didn't want to go to work and slowed my steps as I walked toward the bullpen. Some mornings I barely made it inside the pen before the guard closed the gate. Just as he was shutting the gate, I would run and leap through before he slammed it closed. He'd give me a look, then turn and push his way through the crowds of prisoners as he headed for the front of the pen. There have been days, however, when my gamble didn't pay off, and the guard had locked the gate be-fore I got there. Those times I was sent to the hole. Those little cells are one-man boxes. Their only furnishings were a steel toilet, metal sink, and a sheetless plastic mattress laid on an iron bunk. I have spent days, sometimes weeks, in those cells waiting to be called before the disci-plinary board, whose punishment was often making me work an extra eight days in the field. Though I knew the penalty for being late to the pen, it was never enough motivation for me to hurry. Like every pris-oner, I worked all week so I could be able to enjoy my weekends how I wanted to. But there were times when the field work would get to me. I got tired of it and I would refuse to rush myself out to the bullpen. Whether I had to cut grass or pick vegetables, the field work wasn't easy. When that sun was out and I was bent over a hoe scraping the ground, sweat stinging my eyes and muscles aching, there were plenty of times I wanted to stop and tell the line pusher to call the truck to bring me in. But when I had pushed myself to finish the work, the line pusher constantly riding his horse up and down past me, yelling and watching while I worked, aggravated me. It was knowing I had to put up with the sun, muscle cramps, and the line-pusher each day that often slowed my steps to the bullpen and made the hole seem like a spring vacation.

Inside the bullpen I would stand and listen to the morning gossip between prisoners. I remember one morning the talk was about a young prisoner who had been raped the night before in one of the other dorms. Even in this world where men are mentally and emotionally tormented, hearing about the physical suffering of another prisoner still fascinates most. I was no different. I listened to their conversation.

"I bet he was good?"

"Was he! I couldn't get myself all the way in before I shot off." He paused as if to replay the sexual moment in his head, then said, "Damn."

The men laughed.

"Say," another one spoke. "How's his body?"

"Man, he ain't got no tattoo or other spot on his body," the prisoner said. "And it's sooo soft."

"Yeah!" came an excited response. "I got three packs for some of that tonight."

"Let me enjoy him a few nights first." At that, all of them laughed.

At that, I shook my head. I felt sympathy for the prisoner who had become a prison whore, a title he carries with him for the rest of his time in prison. Like a fugitive, he will be stalked by other prisoners wanting him to take care of "their business." Some will pay him, some won't. Some will treat him kindly, some won't. Some will talk about him, and some won't. But to lure them all from all their material possessions he will politely wave and smile as he swishes by them in tight jeans so they can see the lining of his homemade bikini underwear.

There are prisoners who will swear that they will never "mess around" with a whore. But the loneliness of prison and the longing for female companionship gets to every prisoner, and you find some of them in the company of a whore laughing, talking, and peeping at the whore's butt as he walks away. Some will even wait to catch the whore alone to request a sexual favor that will be a guarded secret between them. Eventually, there will be prisoners fighting over the whore. And there will be one prisoner who will offer the whore a chance to live respectfully by becoming a prison wife. If the whore accepts the invitation, then it is said that the whore has "chosen" his "man." But as a wife the whore won't have any say about his own life. He will only do what his man wants, participate only in the activities his man is involved in, and wish for nothing beyond his man's dreams. He will be trapped in a prison inside a prison. When he showers he must face the corner, sit down on the toilet when he urinates, make his man's bed, fold his clothes, and prepare canteen food for him to eat at night. He won't be allowed to talk to another prisoner outside of his man's presence, and then he gives only a smiling hello. Beyond this he will sit quietly and wait for when his man decides to have sex with him. He can't say no, because that is the life he "chose." For providing comfort, companionship, and sex to his man, the man will protect him from physical attacks, provide food, clothes, cosmetics, and shower the wife with gifts. To my astonishment I have witnessed in these prison marriages that the man treats his prison wife better than the woman he was married to.

I stood there thinking about the sickness of this place and shook my head.

The guard had made it up to the front of the bullpen and slid the gate back. "Hold the noise!" he yelled. The noise in the pen began to grow quiet.

Holding a metal clipboard, he yelled, "Answer up when I call your number."

"46 89 44."

"Here."

"33 63 74."

"Yeah." I answered and walked through the gate behind the other prisoners, picked up a hoe, and stood in line next to another prisoner.

The line pusher rode his horse down beside us counting, when he stopped next to me. I hated him. Most of the other prisoners in the line didn't like him either. His father had worked at Angola for thirty years and now was retired, but he was nothing like his father. He was arrogant, and when he spoke, you could tell by his voice how much he detested us.

"Say Hopper"—my name is Harper, something he could never say correctly—"You gonna work today."

I squinted my eyes up at him and lifted my hand to block the sun. He was a skinny kid with a clean shaven face, and his black hair was cut to the military length. He never wore his prison uniform. Instead he enjoyed wearing green camouflage fatigues with black combat boots, maybe because it made him feel like a drill sergeant at boot camp. He sure worked us that way.

Angola, these eighteen acres of farmland, was all he knew. He was born here and raised in this farm. And he had lived out his entire life within Angola's borders. Anywhere beyond this place was foreign to him and to travel off of this land would leave him lost. He was a man without skill, without significance, without any purpose in the world besides Angola. And my misery gave him his purpose.

"I came out the gate, didn't I?" I snapped.

He looked at me and grinned. "Yep," he said. "Today's gonna be a good day." He then kicked his horse in the side with his heel, and the horse carried him toward the front of the line.

I soon heard him holler, "Walk it!" and we started to move. For a moment, I thought about turning around and going to the hole, but as I kept getting further away from the prison that thought died.

There was not a cloud in the sky as we walked down a dirt road. The bright sun made us sweat so that as our feet kicked up dirt from the road, dust stuck in our hair, on our faces and arms and clothes. Arriving at the field, we looked like we were coming out of a dust storm.

At the field site the line pusher decided not to call numbers from the roster. It took too long, he said, and he wanted to get as much work out of us as he could. Instead, he rode his horse down beside us, pointing at us and calling out a number.

After he had given all of us a number, he yelled out, "I want you to go down those rows and pull up those soybean trees. Don't leave none of the roots in the ground. .After you pull the trees up, lay them in the rows' gutters. You got fifteen minutes. When I holler, 'Swing it around,' you'd best be finished. Now get to work."

We laid our hoes in a pile on the ground and walked to our rows.

I looked at the field. All I could see were mile-long rows of dead bushes. Some of the bushes' dry leaves had fallen on the ground and crackled under my feet as I stepped on them going halfway into the row and started pulling up the bushes. Though the bushes were dead, their roots were firmly in the ground, and pulling them up was not an easy task. Catching a bush by its stalk, I had to yank, lean backwards and pull, twist, and then yank at it again as the bush popped out of the ground. If some of the roots were still in the ground, I had to get on my knees and dig into the dirt with my fingers to pull them out. Then I got up and went to the next bush.

After pulling sixteen bushes up, I was tired. My shoulders and back ached. Splinters from the stalks were stuck under the skin of my hands, I had streaks of dirt on my pants legs where I had wiped my hands a few times, and sweat turned dirt on my arms to mud. I stood up and looked at how much I still had to do. Some prisoners were already finished with their rows and were standing at the end of the field waiting for the line pusher to move us to a new set of rows. They had gotten lucky. Their rows didn't have as many bushes on them as mine, a fact our line pusher would not take into consideration when it was time to swing. I got back to work.

I had three bushes to go when I heard the line pusher holler, "Swing 'er around."

As the other prisoners began walking to their other rows, I hurried to pull the last three bushes up, leaving their roots in the ground. I then jogged down to my next row.

On that row, I worked faster at pulling out the bushes. I'm not sure whether I was motivated by wanting to finish quickly so I could get a breather, or whether I was hoping the day would just be over—probably both. If the bushes' roots were not sticking out of the ground after I pulled out the bush, I left the roots there and just kicked a little dirt in the hole and moved on to the next bush. Being able to create ways to "get over" from doing all of the required work is a necessary art in the field to avoid getting sent to the hole.

I made it to the end of my row before most of the other prisoners. I stood catching my breath when I noticed the line pusher riding towards me.

"Say Hopper," he said, stopping his horse in front of me. "You through with your row?"

I wondered whether he was asking me a trick question. I wasn't sure if he saw the roots I left when he rode down and he was asking to see if I would lie, or whether he was just picking on me. I knew that if I said

I wasn't finished, he would ask me what I was doing standing up, then send me to the hole. But if I told him that I was through and he had proof I was lying, he would send me to the hole. The only chance I had to save myself was to get him talking about something else.

"When are you planning to give us a break?" I asked him.

"What's that?" he snapped.

"A break, " I repeated. "When do you plan on giving us one?"

"You're speaking for the line, Hopper?"

"Nope. I'm just asking."

"Well, since you're just asking," he said, smiling at me, "I'm gonna give you a break right now." Then he hollered, "Swing 'er round!"

"What?" I said. "You got guys still pulling bushes out of their rows. It's hot out here. You're not supposed to work us in this heat without a break. You can call the truck—" My voice went out of control.

He grinned, proud that he had gotten to me. He kicked at his horse and rode back up to the front of the field yelling, "Swing 'er round!" "Swing 'er round!"

I let out a sigh, then slowly walked over to the next row.

As I worked pulling up the bushes, I thought about the man I pushed in the wheelchair, and the possibility of dying here weighed on me. Then my mind drifted to the life I left. Society thinks that the work gets to us. But the work is nothing compared to thoughts of family and how badly we miss them, the lonely and distressed feeling there is in sharing holidays and birthdays over the phone, the heat that comes in your throat when your child or the person you love looks into your face and asks when you're coming home, but you can't answer them because you don't even know. The truths can't be suppressed and your thoughts are constantly rambling from feelings of hopelessness to confused thoughts of giving up… this is the hardest labor.

"Heaad Lineee!" the line pusher hollered. It was time to go in.

We lined up and headed back to the prison. When I got back to my dorm, I took off my boots and sat on the floor beside my bed, massaging my feet. I was relieved the day was over with. Soon a whistle blew. It was time to eat.

Chapter 9

At some point you say that's enough. You get tired. As you sit in your bed staring around at the dormitory of prisoners laughing, some playing dominos, while others sit by their beds talking or writing, you think about the routines and sickness of this place, and of how your entire life has been reduced to two steel locker boxes and a bunk. You realize that you live from one sunrise to the next with nothing more to look forward to than a change on the dinner menu and for yard calls. This mental grind forces you to a decision. You have to set yourself free to survive. Either you're going to accept the lot life has thrown you, make peace with it, and live it out as best you can, or try making peace with yourself only to realize that you can't, so you walk around angry until you snap. My point of decision started on a day when I was coming out of the field.

We had been out picking strawberries and I had put a few of them in the potato chip bag I had brought with me to drink water in. As I was walking through the bullpen gate, guards patted us down. This was routine; they wanted to make sure none of us was carrying pipes, rods, or anything that could be turned into a knife.

I walked up to a guard, holding my arms up, turned around, and he patted my pants leg, on my pockets, and around my waist, finding the bag of strawberries.

"What's this?" he asked, taking the bag and opening it. "Ah, strawberries."

I explained to the guard that there were only seven strawberries in the bag and I was going to put some sugar on them to eat at lunch. He glanced down at the open bag and shrugged, "What you gonna give me for them?"

"C'mon, it's only seven."

The guard laughed. "But they're my strawberries."

This particular guard carried one of the big names that ran Angola for decades. He was raised on this farm; "a B line baby," we prisoners called him among ourselves. He later climbed rapidly through the ranks to become an assistant warden. There was a certain smug attitude such men of his status possessed.

I looked into his eyes and knew I didn't have an argument. If he wanted to, he could write me up and send me to the hole because I was not supposed to bring in anything I picked. Nevertheless, I made an effort to persuade him.

"They didn't feed us anything for breakfast," I said, "and I just wanted something sweet with my lunch."

"How I know that?" he told me. "You might was going to make some beer with them."

"I was going to eat them."

"You say."

I knew where our conversation was headed. "C'mon, seven strawberries. That ain't nothing to do anything with."

"You want 'em."

"How much?"

He opened the bag to look at the strawberries again. "Bring a cold drink out with you the next half."

"What kind?" I asked, defeated. "I only got root beer and Dr. Pepper."

"Dr. Pepper," he told me. "And a bag of chips." Then he tossed the bag of strawberries on the ground and waved me past him.

I accepted this bullying to avoid a write-up. I went to my dorm thinking, I can't even eat a strawberry. After I picked them! That realization bothered me all afternoon.

Later that evening I got dressed to attend a church service in the prison's chapel. When I arrived I learned that the service was being conducted by prisoners. I tried to leave but was forced to stay because the guard watching over the service had already turned his count in. The prisoners put on a jubilant exercise of dancing, clapping, and singing, and I found myself on my feet clapping along. Then, the prisoner preacher rose from his chair behind the pulpit to deliver his sermon.

He looked out over the audience of prisoners and asked low, "What type of God we serve?" Then raising his voice into the pulpit's microphone, he repeated, "What type of God we serve?" Stretching his arms out to the congregation, he answered, "A big and mighty God."

"Amen," someone in the crowd shouted.

"And I don't believe our big God saved us to kill us in Angola. He wants us free." The prisoners nodded in agreement. "Free in sprit and free in the world. And can't no devil at no courthouse box against what God want for his children. Freedom, I say, Freedom. God demands Pharaoh to let us go."

Some of the prisoners leaped to their feet, yelling, "Preach! Preach!"

"If God is for us, who can be against us? He said, 'Ask and it shall be given,' so I petition God today to deliver his children from bondage."

The prisoners stood clapping, "Amen! Amen!" After several minutes the clapping died down and the prisoners started singing "Precious Lord."

I still remember that atmosphere. It was pleasant, genuine. After the service I stood outside the chapel waiting for the guard to tell us the count was clear so I could go back to my dorm when an older black prisoner approached me and asked whether I enjoyed the service.

"I liked it," I said. "This is the first time I have attended a prisoner-led service."

"I'm glad you enjoyed it." He then asked me how long I had been going to church.

"In Angola?" I asked. "Or on the street?"

"Since you've been alive."

"Oh, all my life," I said. "I been in church Monday through Sunday since I was a kid."

"That's good. "Then you will come back."

I smiled. "I don't know. I might."

"Well, think about it." And then he walked away and began talking to other prisoners.

The next afternoon I saw that same prisoner on the rec yard walking by himself. We cut our eyes at each other but didn't speak.

A week later I went back to that service. Just as before when I walked through the chapel door, the music was loud. I clapped, laughed, and rocked to the music in my seat. And when it got time for the prisoner to preach, I stood with the other prisoners to sing "Amazing Grace"; I waved my hands in the air, and with my eyes closed, swayed side to side, when I heard someone say in my ear, "I'm glad you're back," and I opened my eyes and saw that same prisoner I had met at the last service standing beside me.

After the service we talked briefly and over the next few days he kept coming around me: on the walk, at work, walking the rec yard. He even came and sat with me in the kitchen. The more he came around me, the more suspicious I became of him. Here was a man old enough to be my dad who had never spoken to me in his life wanting to always be around me. I had been around the prison enough to know that the older prisoners were not to be trusted, and he had already been incarcerated 30 years. So I made certain to keep a barrier up between us whenever he came around. I knew that if he had any mischievous motives, my off-handedness would drive him to frustration so that would either make him stop coming around me or make him reveal his true intentions, hoping I would submit to them. Knowing that the latter was a greater likelihood, I had to be ready with a response.

One afternoon we were walking around the rec yard talking about our cases and the likelihood of us ever leaving Angola when finally he opened up about why he kept coming around me. It was a subliminal statement, expressed by him saying that he had resolved he wasn't going anywhere. "I'm here," he told me, which suggested I might as well accept the reality of this statement too and start making a life for myself behind these walls.

"Never," I told him. "I love myself too much to give up. Plus, I got family out there that still care about me." I said this because he had none. Over the years, after his mother died, his other family members began to slowly distance themselves from him until finally their visits stopped, he received no more mail from them, and they changed their phone numbers. He was left alone in this world of Angola. As a result he had grown distant, untrusting, suspicious, and his internalized anger showed on his face. In his search to feel that his life mattered to others, he turned to the environment around him. He boxed for the prison, played football with other prisoners, and helped the recreation guard manage the prisoner softball teams. Immersing himself in the prison sports, he found an arena where he felt needed, and you could tell this was how he saw himself when he talked about his prison sports accomplishments. But I observed two things whenever he opened his mouth. One was that prison became all he knew. He could not hold a conversation at length beyond what went on in Angola. The other was that time and absence of family had convinced him that there was nothing for him outside Angola. He was now at home, and he stood trying to convince me to accept his reasoning as his own.

"You say you got family that love you," he said. "They send you any money?"

"No."

"They come visit you?"

"Too far to drive."

"Has anybody in your family gotten you a lawyer?"

"My mom can't afford one," I said. "But that don't mean my mom don't love me 'cause she hasn't bought me a lawyer."

"Umm," he said. "Your mom won't get you a lawyer to help you get out, but she says she loves you. If that's love, I wouldn't want to experience her hate."

That was typical in all our discussions. No matter what we talked about, he was sure to take a negative view in them. And without noticing it, being more around him, I began to feel that I was doomed in this place. I shall never forget one afternoon I was lying on my bunk thinking about my case. "I didn't pull the trigger," I said to myself. "The one that did got out after seven years, and I'm doing life because he lied telling the jury I was with him." I grew angry thinking about this. I looked around the dorm at the prisoners playing their radios loud, laughing, eating, talking, and I became so enraged at them that I wished a bomb would drop, killing them all, because I felt they were good for nothing. Wasted sperm, I called them.

As I lay in my bunk taking in the scene around me, my anger turned to hurt, hurt that I could not rely on anyone to help me get out, and hurt that my life was wasting away in Angola. If only my mom could hit the lottery. My hurt became frustration and this caused such a feeling of urgency in me that I got out of my bed, went to the phone, and dialed my mother's number. I was ready to unleash my hurt, anger, and frustration at her. I was ready to let her know that if she wasn't going to help me, I wouldn't continue calling. I was ready. But when her soft voice came through the receiver, I quickly remembered she was my mother, and I couldn't bring myself to unload my grief on her. Inside of me I knew that if she was able she would go broke for me. I held the phone talking to her, tears welling up in my eyes.

As our conversation came to a close, I heard my little niece Trinity hollering in the background. I asked my mother what was the matter with her.

"Your niece wants to talk to you," she said.

"Put her on," I said, and my mother placed the phone to Trinity's little mouth.

"He-ey."

"You know who this is?"

"Ye-ah."

"Who?"

"Unc Fa Fa."

"I love you."

"I love you too," and then she said the three words I have never forgotten. "You my hero." Those words vibrated through me.

"What you said?" I asked her anxiously. "You said I'm your hero?"

"Ye-ah."

My mother's voice came back through the receiver. She was laughing, proud that her granddaughter was learning to talk.

"You heard her?" she asked me.

"Yes, I heard her," I answered. When I told her I had heard Trinity, I knew she was talking only about Trinity's words, but through my niece's words I had heard something more. We said our good-byes and hung up the phone. I went and laid in my bed and thought about my niece's words.

Her simple words had opened a door in me that I didn't realize I had closed. Prison had consumed me. From the moment of my arrest, all I ever focused on was me. Who was going to help me get out of the mess

I found myself in? I never once stopped and thought about who I had hurt. Sure, I have often reminded myself of the family I left and how I wished I was with them to help out. But I never saw their hurt. It wasn't until my niece spoke her simple words that I saw my family's pain and I realized that, through my incarceration, they suffered too.

The next afternoon I went on the rec yard and saw that same prisoner who kept coming around me shadow-boxing by himself, and as I stood, something opened up in me watching him. He was hopeless, bitter, alone, an Angola relic. Did I really want to end up like him? I had tried everything I could, yet nothing I tried on my own did me any good. And so, that night at church, for the first time in my life I cried sincerely for God's presence. And for the first time, I felt Him.

Over the next days and weeks that prisoner and I would talk, and I saw him becoming attached to me. He follows me around everywhere, even to church. He has told me that I was the most intelligent person he had ever met, that was why he liked being around me. I knew, however, that in his mind he had placed me as his "family," and there was nothing I could say to stop his sick ideas. I know he has even gone around secretly telling people that we were a couple, and he probably wonders why I haven't bothered to confront him. Whenever I do think about him and his sickness I am reminded of Paul in 2 Corinthians 12:7-9 where he wrote of a thorn in his side to remind him of God's grace. Then my niece's words come back to my remembrance as though they are God's spirit counseling me that my life is not all about me, and that He loved me even when I didn't deserve His love. Therefore, I must love even when the person doesn't deserve to be loved.